Take One as Needed

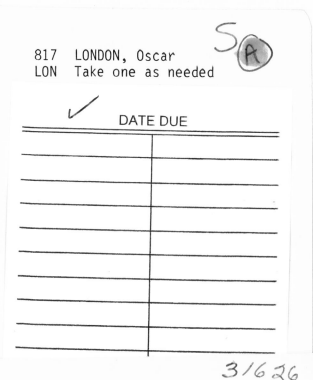

Take One as Needed

50 CAPSULES OF HUMOR
FOR TEMPORARY RELIEF
OF MISERY DUE TO
LOW-FAT DIETS, SAFE SEX,
& AEROBIC EXERCISE.

Oscar London, M.D., W.B.D.

Ten Speed Press
Berkeley, California

Most of the stories in this book appeared in one or another of the following publications:
San Francisco Chronicle Sunday Punch
San Francisco Magazine
San Francisco Focus Magazine
Los Angeles Times Sunday West Magazine
Coast FM & Fine Arts
Look Magazine

1☉
Ten Speed Press
P.O. Box 7123
Berkeley, California 94707

Cover design by Fifth Street Associates
Book design by Seventeenth Street Studios
Typeset by Wilsted & Taylor

Library of Congress Catalog Card Number: 88-051844
ISBN 0-89815-297-6

Printed in the United States of America

1 2 3 4 5 — 93 92 91 90 89

To
Joan

CONTENTS

AND NOW FOR A HEALTHY DOSE OF REALITY

Antidepressants

1 PRESCRIPTION FOR LOVE

WHEN I met Linda, I was taking Valium, one tablet before each meal and two at bedtime. By coincidence, she was also on Valium, one tablet before each meal and two at bedtime.

On our first date, we fell calmly in love.

Before long, I was down to one tablet twice daily, and she had to take only a half tablet every now and then, as needed, for relaxation.

When our romance grew more feverish, I began taking a multivitamin stress tab once daily before breakfast, and she went back on Valium, one tablet before each meal and two at bedtime.

Every Friday and Saturday night, I wined her and dined her. After a few weeks, she grew chubby and my ulcer flared up. She began taking an appetite suppressant, one capsule daily on arising, and I started taking Maalox, two tablespoons one hour after each meal and at bedtime.

On a skiing weekend, we both came down with deep chest colds, and the resort doctor placed us on elixir of terpin hydrate with codeine, one teaspoon every four hours, as needed, for cough.

It was great sitting around the fire in the lodge, sipping our terpin hydrate and dreaming our little dreams.

At Christmas, we exchanged pillboxes. We announced our engagement in February. Two days before the wedding, she got into a terrible argument with her mother over the invitation list and broke out in the worst case of hives her doctor had ever seen. He prescribed an antihistamine capsule every eight hours and renewed her Valium prescription, one tablet before each meal and two at bedtime. The next day, she disappeared.

I received a postcard from her a week later stating that she had eloped with her pharmacist.

I am presently taking an antidepressant, two capsules before each meal and three at bedtime. So far, they haven't worked.

2 A HOSPITAL BILL TO DIE OVER

*T*o the cognoscenti, Moffitt is the Paris Ritz of San Francisco hospitals. Moffitt is the only hospital I know of that offers valet parking to ambulances. Last month, Robin Leach, in a departure from his usual format, had himself rushed to Moffitt's Emergency Room for a TV special entitled, "Death Styles of the Rich and Famous," only to find himself alive and well in the parking lot fifteen minutes later with an 800 calorie diet sheet in his hands.

I recently had the privilege of spending five days at Moffitt Hospital with an admitting diagnosis of "acute abdominal pain," arguably the most prestigious disorder in Cecil's *Textbook of Medicine*. You wouldn't think a five-day stay in a semi-private room could add up to $413,409.12, would you? How, you might ask, could a simple case of "gas" inflate, as it were, to this preposterous figure? Let me tell you a little secret: the bill would have been *twice* that amount if I hadn't signed out "AMA" (Against Medical Advice).

First, there was the three A.M. rush to the Emergency Room by ambulance—$1,912.00, including Special Effects (pulsating siren, blinking lights, squealing brakes), plus taxes, license, floor mats, and delivery.

Inside the E.R., I told the intern my belly ached. He asked how long I had been having "abdominal pain" and I foolishly said, "About six hours." That came to a penalty fee of $14,200.00 to cover "standard hourly rates for pain and suffering that could have profitably been spent in hospital if patient had summoned ambulance at onset of symptoms, instead of waiting six hours."

I was then instructed to undress. The admitting nurse took

one look at me and ordered me to redress ($856.00 for "change of dressings"). An orderly helped me into a skimpy gown open at the back ($2,499.99—fully *five times* what you'd pay for the same *shmata* at the Neiman-Marcus clearance center in Oakland).

The radiologist discovered an abnormal collection of gas in my descending colon and an accountant was rushed to the hospital for consultation. At the eleventh hour, it was decided that $37,100.00 was not asking too much for what doctors call a "working diagnosis."

I was admitted to a semi-private room ($5,300.00 per day, inclusive of facial tissue, plastic comb, and toothbrush). My roommate was a red-bearded, 300-pound motorcyclist freaked out on Angel Dust and suffering separation anxiety from his bike. All night, at the top of his lungs, he called out "KAWA-SAKI! " As luck would have it, his nurse's name was Michiko Kawasaki and between the two of them—he shouting "KAWA-SAKI" and she running into the room, crying "YES? YES?"—I spent a sleepless night.

Oh, how I spent! In the end, I figured at 5,300 bucks a day, why be unconscious for eight hours?

In the morning, I still had my belly ache. A male nurse appeared with a bottle of '88 Cutter, *Premier Cru*, 5% Glucose in Normal Saline. In the finest tradition of sommeliers, the nurse presented the label for my approval before hanging the bottle upside down to preserve its cork. Then, with a deft motion of his wrist, he inserted a #20-gauge needle into a vein on my left arm. Although a bit sweet, with a lingering salty after-taste, the '88 Cutter Glucose in Saline had a wonderfully prismatic luminescence—a steal at $1,712.00 a liter.

Shortly after one P.M. on my second hospital day, the heart of my stressed-out roommate suddenly stopped beating. Code Blue! A frantic team of cardiologists, anesthesiologists, nurses, and loan officers from a major California bank dashed into the room. With the possible exception of St. Bartholomew's in London, no hospital gives better Code Blue than Moffitt.

Within three minutes, my roommate's heart was beating with the regularity of Big Ben, complete with the sonorous BONG on the hour. I was charged almost two thousand bucks in cover charges, but, hey, who's complaining?

Three days passed—and so did my gas. I'm not sure how the doctors and nurses did it—or whether they were even aware of it—but on my fourth hospital day, I was pain-free! Perhaps it was the threat of surgery that precipitated me into good health.

I knew surgery was being contemplated when, at two in the morning of my third hospital day, I was paid an emergency bed-side visit by the Assistant Finance Minister of Argentina. He was *muy simpático!* He offered to share a sizable portion of his country's outstanding foreign debt with me should I survive "a certain proposed intervention." There were genuine tears in his eyes as I pleaded, "Don't cry for me, Argentina."

Five hours later, without benefit of surgery, I was a healthy man. Since no one seemed able to cope with a sudden turn for the better in a hospital bed, I signed out the next day, AMA.

Two nights after I sent my bill for $413,409.12 to my insurance carrier, I awoke at three A.M. to find a blue cross burning on my front lawn.

Undaunted, I'm determined to pay in full my debt to Moffitt Hospital. In the meantime, I'm scratching out a living playing the California Lottery. I figure if I can hit just two Instant Wins, I can not only retire my debt to Moffitt, but maybe have a little left over to donate to my favorite charity: The Physician's Relief Fund for Disabled Malpractice Lawyers.

3 THE DARING YOUNG MAN ON THE FLYING BASKET CHAIR

*T*HE greatest difficulty I have in shopping at Cost Plus Imports is keeping my hands off the merchandise. By nature, I am a tinkler of wind chimes, a honker of brass horns, a thunker of temple gongs. I am a strummer of samisens, a tapper of wafer tins, a pincher of sales girls. I am, in short, a damn nuisance in the eyes of the Cost Plus power structure.

My first serious brush with C.P. management stemmed from the Hanging Basket Chair Incident of two years ago:

While taking a few practice swings with an Igorot headhunter's axe in the toy department one Saturday morning, I caught sight, across the store, of what appeared to be a man-sized wicker womb depending from a chain attached to the ceiling. I found myself curiously drawn to the chair. I thrust the axe and its instruction manual into the hands of a male customer whose wife was nagging him, and clawed my way through a living wall of tourists until I stood before the gently swaying seat.

With an agile backward leap, I mounted the basket chair and was soon swinging merrily to and fro like the Focault's Pendulum at the Planetarium. I discovered that by kicking my legs out vigorously, I could increase the distance of each succeeding arc traversed by the chair. In no time, thanks to the long chain and my strong calf muscles, I became, in effect, a human wrecking ball.

As my swinging chair struck the top of counter #12 in the adjacent department, a 92-piece set of Noritake china was transformed into a 4,306-piece set of Noritake china. At the opposite end of our arc, in Household Decorations, we explosively demolished 813 ornamental glass balls blown in Taiwan. Frantically, I twisted my hurtling body to change our course and quickly brought about the downfall, in Southeast Asia Notions, of counters #6, 5, 4, 3, 2, and 1, which fell like a row of dominoes. The din of crashing glass, aluminum, copper, pewter, and brass was almost drowned out by the screams of tourists. Once my initial guilt and air sickness had subsided, I found myself taking no small measure of glee in the sensation I was creating.

The store manager tried to approach me but was cut down by a stampede, off counter #14, of 985 carved water buffaloes from Kenya, ranging in size from 98¢ to $800.00. His assistant, a young man whose turquoise-dyed hair had turned snow-white in the preceding five minutes, leaped into the breach and demanded,

"Sir, dismount this instant!"

"Not by the chair on your chainy-chain-chain!" I cried, wildly kicking my legs and soaring to new heights.

"In that case," announced the assistant manager, side-stepping a bombardment of piñatas, "I shall have to resort to forcible extraction. Yo, Matt! Come over here!"

Matt, an over-zealous floor manager on his way up, charged my basket chair like Refrigerator Perry closing in on a tackle dummy. As his arms wound tightly about the wicker back of my seat, his feet left the ground and Matt, the over-zealous floor manager, was on his way up, up, up. At the apogee of our impromptu Gemini flight, his weight plus mine caused the chain to snap.

Just before the re-entry of my wicker capsule, Matt took his walk in space. He landed face-down across a narrow table marked "50% Off" and was promptly snapped up by a pair of elderly sisters visiting from Quincy, Illinois.

Meanwhile, down came baby, cradle and all. Luckily, my fall was cushioned by an enormous consignment of either assorted wax fruit from Hong Kong or hand-dipped candles from Taipei—the distinction is academic.

The final list of damages reads like the Far Eastern edition of the Sears Roebuck Catalog, plus the last stanza of *The Twelve Days of Christmas*. After I promised to confine my future activities at Cost Plus to tinkling wind chimes and strumming samisens, the power structure sent me a bill for $7,846.29. One thing you've got to say for the guys who run Cost Plus Imports—they sure give a guy his money's worth.

4 MASTER FORGER OF BLACK VELVET PAINTINGS ARRESTED IN OAKLAND

A musician must make music, an artist must paint, a poet must write, if he is to be ultimately at peace with himself. What a man can be, he must be. Abraham Maslow

*B*RUNO Bonaventura steps back from the black velvet painting on his easel. "Perfekko!" he growls in self-approval. The 300-pound, fifty-seven-year-old master forger has done it again—painted a kneeling, bronze-skinned maiden wearing naught but a red hibiscus in her hair. So skillful are his forgeries that they could readily pass for *original* black velvet paintings found in boutiques south of the Equator across the world.

Mounted in a handsome frame of simulated teak, a Bonaventura forgery might fetch upwards of thirty dollars on the black velvet black market. Maybe more.

For years, Bonaventura cut a wide swath in San Francisco's financial district as a highly respected bike messenger. On his fiftieth birthday, he impulsively pawned his sturdy Schwinn and booked passage on a cruise ship bound for Tahiti. A latter-day Gauguin, he fell instantly in love with the languid tropics.

Purchasing a bolt of black velvet and a box of Day-Glo paint, Bonaventura discovered that he had a God-given talent for painting in the native style, but his work was patently derivative. Tragically, he concluded that if he wanted to remain in his beloved Tahiti, he would have to forge the work of local artists and, as they say in the tropics, palm off his ersatz schlock as the genuine article. He soon found a ready tourist market for his marked-down nudes. The rest, as they say, is velvet.

After seven years, he was banished from Paradise for flooding the market and discrediting the validity of black velvet as a reputable artistic medium. Bonaventura went into seclusion in Oakland.

When uniformed agents of the art forgery division of Interpol broke into Bonaventura's motel room in Oakland just before dawn on March 20th, 1988, they were astounded to find the walls covered with dozens of luminous, perfectly ghastly black velvet paintings (estimated sidewalk value: in excess of $400).

Dressed in an orange jumpsuit, the rotund master forger lay face down on a black velvet blanket covering the king-sized motel bed. Slowly, he opened one eye and, a short time later, the other, to find his bed surrounded by seven men wearing berets, thin black mustaches, and artists' smocks. Instead of holding palettes, the gaunt, pale men brandished Uzis. Sighing massively, Bonaventura resumed sleeping.

"Don't move!" cried the head agent to the unconscious artist while a subordinate took a Polaroid picture of the suspect. Labeled Exhibit A, the snapshot resembles nothing so much as a Bonaventura forgery of a bloated Hawaiian sun setting ponderously over an ink-black sea—another example of Nature (or Bonaventura) copying Art.

The agents began removing the black velvet paintings from the walls but stopped when the motel manager rushed in bearing papers authenticating the works as originals. It was in the motel room's closet and the suspect's van parked outside that agents uncovered the huge cache of genuine Bonaventura forgeries: Over 200 paintings on every subject under the tropical sun—coconut palms silhouetted against Pacific sunsets, bare-chested young men in Hawaiian war canoes, glass balls in fishing nets, sailboats drifting in dark lagoons, plus 181 studies of an unclad, kneeling maiden winking enigmatically over her left shoulder.

Extradited to Portugal, Bonaventura stood trial in Lisbon for international fraud. He categorically denied that he forged black velvet paintings.

Rather, he claimed, he *restored* black velvet paintings. Paintings on velvet, he pointed out, require periodic vacuuming and dry-cleaning. Otherwise, after about ten years, they lose their luster and need major restoration. Bonaventura's lawyers offered in evidence the affadavits of hundreds of satisfied patrons who, through the years, had sent the artist their faded sunsets and brunettes.

The judge leaned forward and asked the defendant, "Señor Bonaventura, how much, on the average, do you charge for a 'restoration'?"

"Oh six, maybe seven dollah."

The judge promptly declared a mistrial and invited Bonaventura into his chambers. There, on black velvet, against the wall behind the judge's desk, was a huge 1920 nude whose sunburn appeared to be peeling.

Using techniques that have been borrowed recently by restorers in the Sistine chapel, Bonaventura painstakingly removed layers of cigarette smoke, beer stains, lint, and paint until he reached pure velvet. He should have stopped at the lint.

Last month, a retrospective of Bonaventura's work was exhibited in Lisbon's Prición Nacional and received mixed reviews.

5 BLOCK MY VIEW, MAKE MY DAY

WHEN I moved to the East Bay hills twenty-five years ago, I had an unobstructed view of a red bridge, a blue bay, a white city, and a green mountain. When I paraded my friends before my picture window, they gasped in awe, writhed in envy and enthused through clenched teeth, "What a marvelous view!" Cryptically they added, "Enjoy it while you can."

The beauty part was that the empty land below my property was part of a municipal park on which nothing had been built for fifty years. Then, nine years ago, through a top-secret operation allegedly involving the release of Berkeley hostages in exchange for arms to Oakland, what was formerly public land below my property became private.

Then cameth the view-busters: the Developers and the Landscape Architects. In a frenzied effort to stop them, I found myself being welcomed at countless city council meetings with the warmth accorded a pit bull in a hospital nursery.

I spent seven agonized years watching my bay view being destroyed piecemeal. By 1985, my picture window framed only the backs of two split-level contemporaries and the rapidly growing branches of six eucalyptus trees. The first split-level wiped out San Francisco, the second obliterated the Golden Gate Bridge. The eucalypti gradually erased Mt. Tam.

The efforts of my formerly envious friends to comfort me were in vain. Like Miss Haversham in *Great Expectations*, I covered my windows with heavy drapes, dressed up in an antique bridal gown and instructed the bakers at Just Desserts not to spare the candles or the cobwebs on my annual birthday cake.

One candle-lit evening last year, while perusing the ads in

the back of a paramilitary magazine, I came across a company known as Homewreckers Anonymous. H.A. specialized in "effecting the disappearance of view-blocking homes—no questions asked."

Done.

The guys at Homewreckers Anonymous did a remarkably efficient job. While the occupants of each split level were on vacation, the Homewreckers hoisted the offending house in the dead of night onto the back of a flat-bed truck and *slowly* made their getaway to a vacant lot in Fairfax. There, the home was sawed into firewood and its contents sold at flea markets.

The Homewreckers spirited the first house away without incident, but apparently came to some grief with the second. On the morning after, a traffic helicopter reporter announced: "Jim, there's a split-level contemporary stalled on east-bound 880 at Appian Way."

To remove the obstructing eucalypti, I contracted with a group of former tree surgeons whose licenses had been revoked due to malpractice. Called the Treeminators, they gave me a choice of three methods of removing the offending vegetation: 1) Defoliation ($300 per tree), 2) Circumferential Bark Strangulation ($400 per tree), 3) Gopher Drop ($500 per tree).

Solely out of curiosity, I chose the Gopher Drop. I'll never forget that sunny morning last October when I looked out at my partially restored view to see—and hear—six towering eucalypti suddenly drop out of sight—*shhhh-WUMP!*

Thanks to the efforts of Homewreckers and Treeminators, I once again enjoy a panoramic bay view; with the help of a sympathetic judge, I was assigned a fourth-floor cell at San Quentin with a sweeping southern exposure. By pressing my face between the bars and squinting, I can sometimes read the time on the Ferry Building clock.

6 ZEN AND THE ART OF LOTTO

WHY do you lose at Lotto while some visitor from Mazatlán wins $24,000,000, using the first six numbers on his Green Card? Why do you lose at Lotto when your mother always told you that you were born to win? Why do you lose at Lotto when you've promised God that if you could win but $3,000,000, you'd be *eternally* grateful?

The reason you lose at Lotto, of course, is impure thinking. At my ashram in Berkeley, I, Baba Reesh Dom Luk, teach Lotto players how to banish impure thinking. For a voluntary contribution of $5.00, you too can learn to approach a Lotto machine with pure thinking.

Do you suppose you can drive up to just any 7-11, saunter over to a Lotto machine and ask the clerk for ten dollars worth of Quick-Pick—and expect to win? Well, often as not, my friends, you will lose. You will lose because your thoughts are impure.

Did you contemplate the *prithma* of the 7-11 as you entered? In other words, had the franchise realized its essential Seven-Elevishment or had it merely achieved *midthra* (Three-Fivishment) and hoped you wouldn't know the difference? Ah, you didn't notice? Your mind, instead, was consumed with an impure thought—consumed, that is to say, with *komonbabi*, or gambling lust.

The clerk adversely reacts to your *komonbabi* as he summons your Quick Pick numbers on the Lotto machine. The Lotto machine, resonating to his negatively charged fingertips, spews out six impure—or losing—numbers.

If you attend my ashram, you will learn that the first two numbers of any winning combination of six reside within your thighs, the middle two numbers separately occupy your hips, and the last two numbers live in your neck. You will learn these winning numbers through meditation, pinching and chanting. Some weeks may pass before your impure thoughts sufficiently lift to allow the winning numbers within your body to become manifest.

Then you will walk humbly into a 7-11 and feel a tingle, say, in one thigh, one hip, and the left side of your neck. Certain of winning $5, you ask the clerk in a supremely indifferent tone of voice, "Ten dollars Quick Pick, please." When the numbers are announced that evening, you will have won $5 unless, of course, some of the tingling you experienced was due to sciatica.

After nine weeks at my ashram, you will approach the Lotto machine, tingling in all six centers. When you ask for ten dollars worth of Quick Pick, the serene clerk will instruct the Lotto machine to spew out 60 random numbers arranged in ten rows of six numbers each. You will go home, undress and bathe. You will don your silk robe with the Lotto 6/49 logo on the back. You will sit down on the couch before the TV set and assume the Lotto's position—legs bent under you, right hand outstretched with palm up. You will empty your head of impure thoughts.

When the winning numbers are flashed on the screen, you will announce to your family and friends that you have a *midrin*, or headache, and must step outside for a little while.

You will walk to the nearest mailbox and post your winning ticket in an envelope addressed to me, Baba Reesh Dom Luk, P.O. Box 7123, Berkeley, CA, 94707. Why must you send me your winning ticket? Because the impurest thought of all is *hol-enchilada*—or greed—and the purest thought of all is *spar-chanji*—or charity.

You might well ask if your winning ticket will be used to enlarge my *vroom vroom* or, as the IRS has termed it, my fleet of Rolls Royces. I can only point out that the path to Enlightenment is an arduous one, calling for a fully independent suspension, rack and pinion steering, a wet bar and disk brakes.

Or would you rather that I, Baba Reesh Dom Luk, drive a Buick?

7 ONE MAN'S RECLINING OVATION

*H*ow can I describe the joy of not attending Obligatory Bay Area Events? The Opera Season, for example, throws me into a frenzy of inactivity. Last year, by exerting heroic neglect, I was able to miss the entire *Ring Cycle*! Knowing the soporific effect of Wagner on San Franciscans, the *Ring*'s director had a professional audience flown in from Düsseldorf to fill the first thirty rows of seats at the Opera House. These seasoned Teutons, in their Ring-side seats, had trained for years to stay awake as long as seventy-two consecutive hours. Bright-eyed and bolt upright, these Bayreuth Aryans displaced our Bay Areans from seats I would normally have given my right arm to refuse to buy.

From all accounts, the armor-plated principals in a Wagnerian opera resemble a Mercedes 450 SEL (the heldentenor) parked facing the grille-work of a BMW 733i (the soprano). For six hours the two hefty sedans gun their motors and honk their horns at one another. Then, a little after one in the morning, they release their brakes and collide in a hideous crash of kettle drums, cymbals, piston rods, rings, valves, and breastplates. A member of the chorus calls AAA and the remains are hauled off to a junkyard in Vallejo (or Valhalla, if you follow the libretto in German). Unlike Siegfried, I wouldn't be caught dead at the Opera.

Nor at the Renaissance Faire. How I look forward each fall to not going to the Faire! To not costuming myself in heavy doublet and chafing pantaloons for a sweaty, dust-choked day of enforced frivolity! To not having teenagers with artificially whitened faces and naturally yellow teeth shout incomprehensible cockneyisms at me! Gadzooks, how I love not going to the Faire!

On a different note, my aversion to singing in public approaches that of seeing my dentist. That's why I stay home and keep my mouth shut during the Sing-Along Messiah. I like to watch the Sing-Along on TV, with the sound turned off. All those flushed, wide-eyed faces, exposing their molars on command! It's as if Oral Roberts had gone into evangelical dentistry and was exhorting his congregation to open their mouths and say "Aaah!" to the Universe. Oh, to be mute, cavity-free and in absentia during the Sing-Along Messiah! Hallelujah! Hallelujah! Hal-le-luuu-jah!

No one in the Bay Area was more saddened than I to learn, several years ago, that the Dickens Faire had actually ceased to exist. No longer could I anticipate the joy of missing the Dickens Faire. (It's no fun not attending something that no longer exists.) But—callooh, callay—last year the Dickens Faire was resurrected. How I love avoiding those bone-chilling, fog-shrouded nights at Fort Mason—some corner of a foreign field that is forever England—where, for an entrance fee of seven dollars, you can queue up for a plate of tasteless bangers and catch a positively Dickensian case of pneumonia.

For weeks before the Bay-to-Breakers Marathon, I sit with my legs dangling anaerobically from a bar stool and contemplate the joys of not running. In my spring training to sit out the Bay-to-Breakers, I may go through half a gallon of Tanqueray in a week. (Tanqueray is the Gatorade of the No Sweat Set.) Next year, while 80,000 Bay Areans are churning their thighs in Golden Gate Park, I plan to curl up on my couch with a thick 19th Century Russian novel and a slim contemporary American poetess.

The trouble is, getting the novel will require me to schlepp to the library. On the other hand, finding a poetess is no problem—I subscribe to a literary club that ships me one each month. Somehow, I never get around to mailing off the card marked, "No poetess next month, please."

8 BANG THE GUN SLOWLY

*H*OLIDAY STATISTIC: So far this year, American TV audiences have been eyewitnesses to the violent deaths of 912 character actors on the major crime shows. The end to this carnage is nowhere in sight.

The leading causes of death on commercial television are gunshot wounds inflicted by "Saturday night specials," although Thursday night re-runs can be quite deadly, too. Besides inflaming the minds of potentially homicidal viewers, this nightly massacre poses considerable casting problems.

The sad fact is that once an actor is killed on TV—especially in prime time—he or she, for all practical purposes, is dead as far as future employment is concerned. Let us cite, for example, the case of a thirty-three-year-old bit player named Delmar Budnip, who is killed in the first scene of a *Midnight Caller* episode in April. When the smoke clears, Budnip picks up his $125.00 check (average sudden-death payoff) and immediately enters the purgatory inhabited by thespians "between roles."

In May, Budnip auditions for the part of a gunshot victim on *Miami Vice*. The casting director takes one look at him and says, "Didn't I see you get plugged on *Midnight Caller*?"

"Yes, but it happened so fast, even my mother didn't recognize me."

"Look, Budnip," says the casting director, "26,000,000 Americans saw you stop a .38-caliber bullet with your forehead last month. Later this year, if they see you getting shot on *Miami Vice*, you're going to put a serious crimp in their suspension of disbelief. Don't you understand? In our murder scenes, we're on the constant lookout for new blood. Why don't you lay low for about a year, let your hair grow long and gain thirty pounds? Then if we need somebody to play a victim knifed in the back, we might call you. Don't call us."

Despondent, Budnip goes to his cold water flat in the Bronx and takes an overdose of Seconal. His girlfriend rushes him to the hospital where the emergency room intern stares at him and says, "Hey, this guy's a dead ringer for a gunshot wound I saw last month."

"That was on TV," explains the girlfriend. "This is for real."

"You mean this character's an *actor*?" says the doctor. "Let me tell you, for an overdose victim he's pretty unconvincing."

With that, Budnip, who hadn't taken more than three capsules, sits bolt upright on his stretcher and sobs, "Dammit, why can't a guy make a decent living dying anymore?"

Oddly enough, in contrast to the victims, the killers on TV have no difficulty landing new roles in their specialty. Last year, Gregory Sleazar, a fiendish young actor from Chicago, shot down a head waiter on *L.A. Law*, strangled three hookers on *Cagney & Lacey*, and shoved a narc off the roof of a condo on *MacGyver*. For an encore, he played a Japanese teppan chef who dices his mother-in-law into half-inch cubes on one of the more puzzling episodes of *Quincy*.

How does Sleazar succeed in getting rehired to commit mayhem while an equally talented actor like Budnip can't get killed again on TV to save his soul?

"It's a simple matter of survival of the fittest," explains Lester Fielding, an assistant casting director for *Murder, She Wrote*. "On TV, once you're dead, you're a has-been. No matter how skillfully you croak, the American public won't tolerate a comeback.

"On the other hand, if the *killer* can live long enough to get arrested, the viewers know he'll probably be out on parole before long. It follows that the reappearance of Sleazar as yet another killer is perfectly acceptable to the viewing public as long as he can come out with his hands up before the last commercial."

Budnip, meanwhile, remains buried in the casting directory. At the present rate of attrition, a critical shortage of victims in relation to killers is developing on television. Soon, the killers on TV will have no choice but to start bumping off one another. The end result, of course, will be the demise of violence on TV. Unless, as unlikely as it sounds, the powers that be take to shooting contestants for refusing to take the gift certificate for $100.

9 THE UNGLUING OF AMERICA

*A*LL over America, small yellow notes are losing their feeble, adhesive grip. Unread, they flutter to the floor. Many of these lost notes say RUSH or URGENT or CALL ASAP or TOP SECRET or I LOVE YOU. The small yellow notes flutter to the floor, unread, and businesses are ruined, hearts are broken, lives are lost.

Our great nation is coming apart at the seams—the center isn't holding. In the old days, our country was united by lasting bonds of paper clips, rubber bands, and Scotch tape. And now in the age of lite beer, lite diets, and lite minds, a lite adhesive is doing us in. The greening of America in the Sixties has been succeeded by the yellowing of America in the Eighties.

A small yellow note flutters to the floor. On it is written the word, SELL. That afternoon the Dow drops more than 500 points.

A small yellow note flutters to the floor. It says, LET'S COOL IT. The next day Gary Hart's campaign for president lies in a shambles.

A small yellow note flutters to the floor. It says, SHRED. Shortly thereafter, Irangate becomes a household word.

A small yellow note flutters to the floor. It says, THIS REFRIGERATOR OFF LIMITS. In the next week, Mrs. Amy Rosenthal of the Bronx gains thirteen pounds.

For years, America has been held together by these small, yellow, gently adherent notes. And now, like dead autumn leaves, they are falling here, falling there, falling everywhere. Soon, the branches of government will be bare; the arms of lovers, empty; the limbs of family trees, fruitless.

Some scientists blame the yellow fallout on the thinning of

the ozone layer. One political analyst is convinced a Soviet satellite dropped the yellow leaflets over America some years ago. He refers to them as "little time bombs that only now are going off."

In retrospect, it was foolish of us to assume that the adhesive backing would never lose its tenuous grip. We ignored the impassioned warnings of the paper clip makers. The tender adhesion of the yellow notes to any surface proved irresistible to consumers. We were stuck on the little stick-ons.

The popularity of the adhesive notes led to major dislocations in other paper-fastener industries. For example, when the president of the nation's second largest staple company saw his profits plummet, he attempted suicide with a staple gun. He survived, but the staples in his forehead activate metal detectors in airports, dooming him to surface transportation for the rest of his life.

What is, perhaps, the most worrisome aspect of the paper fallout is the recent disappearance in the Oval Office of a small yellow note inscribed, "Warning! Mr. President, if you press this button, you can kiss the world goodbye."

10   HOMELESS IN PARADISE

SINCE the average home in Woodsborough sells for $800,000, it is certainly no disgrace to be homeless in that palatial, peninsular community. Greg and Nancy Thorndike are prototypic Puppies—poor urban professionals—who comprise the bulk of Woodsborough's homeless. Both puppies are in their early thirties and work as stockbrokers on Montgomery Street in San Francisco. Their combined income, before taxes, is $47,300, well below the Woodsborough poverty line of 60 K.

Greg and Nancy commute to work in their lovingly maintained, 1973 Jaguar sedan. At night they take turns cruising the tree-lined streets of Woodsborough at a stately fifteen miles per hour. While one drives, the other sleeps. They are required by local ordinance to keep moving or have their homeless status revoked.

The landed gentry of Woodsborough not only were pioneers in recognizing the problem of the Bay Area's homeless, but took an active role in recruiting their own homeless.

According to Mrs. Elisabeth Van Appersbee, Chairperson of the Woodsborough Homeless Society, "Better a darling pair of puppies in a slowly moving Jaguar than a bearded whacko on a runaway skateboard. Once we've admitted a couple like the Thorndikes into the privileged circle of the Homeless of Woodsborough, we of course expect them to help us keep out the riffraff."

Says Nancy Thorndike, "Greg has had to use his stun gun only once to discourage a *nouveau pauvre* couple, up from San Jose."

"Twice," corrects her husband.

The Thorndikes have no illusions of ever being able to afford a home in Woodsborough, but they were among the first of that town's seventeen puppies to apply for emergency shelter. Donated, in part, by a prominent Bay Area architectural firm, each Casa Freebie™ is a sturdy white stucco structure with a red tile roof and just under 800 square feet of floor space. Cost to the Woodsborough Homeless Society: only $98,000 per shelter.

To date, seventeen Casa Freebies™ have been erected in Woodsborough on the spacious grounds of charitable residents. The emergency shelters are designed to resemble either servants' quarters or stables (the Serf or Turf models). According to Mrs. Van Appersby, "The Casa Freebies™ actually tend to enhance the tone of the property. They're not like those dreadful PUP Tents™ that Tiburon has thrown up on the beach for *their* homeless."

To date, Greg and Nancy have had several heated discussions with the architect over the color of the tile in the guest bathroom of their emergency shelter. But they are about to knuckle under and accept the standard hue called Old-Money Green because, as Greg says, "You shouldn't look a gift house in the mouth."

⊶ *11* HUMMM

*M*Y fourteen hundred dollar hi-fi stereo set has developed a hum. It is, indeed, a wonderfully rich and vibrant hum—a real humdinger of a hum, as hums go—but it's a hum nevertheless, and I can't—do you hear me: CAN'T—stand it. Now, if I'd *wanted* a hum to begin with, I almost certainly would have settled for, say, a two or three hundred dollar hum—that is, a relatively humdrum hum—and would have no doubt convinced myself, by and by, that although it was not a great hum, it was a good hum—a hum I could comfortably afford and therefore a restful hum: a kind of ho-hum, as it were. But a fourteen hundred dollar, stereophonic, FM, multiplex, 90 Watt HUMMMM is, for my money, no less than a major acoustic disaster. Especially when you don't know where the humming is coming from. Could it be lurking in my Japanese turntable? In my British receiver? In my German speakers?

I've already written to the various factory representatives. The Japanese firm has humbly suggested that my hum is emanating from my British receiver. The British company has replied, "Humbug!" to the Japanese insinuation and, in turn, has discretely conjectured that the offensive sound might possibly be arising from one or both of the German speakers. The German company, for its part, has taken the novel position that the hum resides solely inside my head and they have urged me to bring my "Hummkopf," as they have diagnosed it, to the attention of a specialist in disorders of the inner ear.

A few days ago, in desperation, I called up the American proprietor of a small radio and TV repair shop in my neighborhood. He promptly came out, listened attentively to my problem, scratched his head for a full minute and finally said, "Hmmmm." That, besides a bill for $15, was all that I was able to get out of him.

Yesterday, as a last resort, I pulled on one of my Army surplus boots and delivered a swift kick to the midsection of my custom-built, oiled-walnut, hi-fi cabinet. To my amazement, the hum began rising gradually in pitch until, within three minutes, it entirely disappeared! My only problem now is that whenever I turn on the set, all the dogs in the neighborhood come running up on my front porch. Frankly, I almost preferred the humming to the barking.

12 RUST IN PEACE

*T*o the serious student of blight, the uglification of America began with the telephone pole, gained momentum with the billboard and peaked with the automobile junkyard. Numberless mountains of twisted, rusting vehicles dot the face of our nation like so many multi-hued warts.

In the eastern suburbs of Los Angeles, a new enterprise—the Park Lawn Automotive Cemetery—is offering fresh hope to lovers of uncluttered landscapes. For the first time in American history, the surviving owner of a totalled vehicle has the opportunity to dispose of the remains with dignity.

A black, chauffeur-driven tow truck, dispatched by radio to the scene of the crack up or break down, will slowly haul your wreck to the cemetery while you and other members of the procession walk behind. At Park Lawn, every effort is made, through the use of modern plastics and touch-up paints, to restore some semblance of pizazz to your former pride and joy.

The directors of Park Lawn make the necessary arrangements for the printing of an obituary in the major dailies. Example:

PACKARD PASSES

A four-door Packard touring car driven by the Arnold Benson family since 1936 passed away yesterday afternoon in the eastbound lane of Highway 24 near Larkmont after a long series of major tune-ups. Surviving are its owners, Mr. and Mrs. Benson, their five children, and the Far Western Fidelity Finance & Loan Co. Services will be held Thursday afternoon in the Little Chapel by the Road at the

Park Lawn Automotive Cemetery. The family asks that in lieu of flowers, donations be sent to AAA.

Services are conducted by a former used car salesman who, so far, has never failed to come up with a few thousand words of praise for the dearly departed. Then, by means of a shrouded derrick, the remains are lowered into a pit, custom-dug to wheelbase specifications. Each grave site is simply and eloquently marked by a thin, gray parking meter signalling the word, EXPIRED.

Fees are reasonable, ranging as they do from $35 down plus $20 monthly for twelve years, all the way up to $6000, cash on the crankcase. The latter price includes a warranty for perpetual care good for 50,000 years or Eternity, whichever elapses first.

Burials are usually well attended, the ranks of the mourners being swelled by somberly dressed representatives of the more enterprising local new car agencies. It is not uncommon, after the funeral, for the bereaved family to be deluged by offers of a lift home in the latest models of any number of makes.

The Park Lawn Automotive Cemetery is presently interring upwards of 500 clients per week and the end, according to president and founder Marcus Buntwell, is nowhere in sight.

"The death knell for the automobile junkyard is being sounded right here and now in Park Lawn," declares Buntwell. "Unfortunately, our waiting list has grown so large that we have a pile of wrecks 60 feet high standing outside our main gate."

To prevent further enlargement of this eyesore, Mr. Buntwell urges that bereft motorists, for the time being, ship the remains of their vehicles, COD, to Detroit or Tokyo with the following bumper sticker: Prepare to Meet Thy Maker.

Sex Hormones

13 A KNIGHT IN SHINING LATEX
Introducing the Whole Body Condom—Not a Moment Too Soon

*T*HE male practitioner of safe sex in 1988 approached his lover only after donning a latex condom, surgical gloves, and a rubber mouth dam. If these precautions had been observed in Shakespeare's time, the following dialogue would have entered the collective consciousness:

JULIET: O Romeo, Romeo! Wherefore art thou Romeo?
ROMEO: Hmmmf! Nnnnmmmnn! Hmmmnnn!

Today's Juliet takes one look at her rubberized Romeo, grabs her attaché case and runs screaming into the streets. Small wonder ladies would rather interface with gentlemen in the board room than have intercourse with them in the bedroom!

In order to improve his image in the boudoir, ever-vain, ever-cautious modern man is about to take the next logical step: the handsome, user-friendly, Whole Body Condom (WBC). Hoping to gain FDA approval, manufacturers of WBC's are feverishly experimenting with prototypes from Europe.

Poland was the first country to test a WBC. Made of triple strength latex and roguishly fashioned to resemble a sixteenth century suit of armor, the Polish tried it out on 200 heterosexual volunteer couples. After one year, the Poles discovered that conscientious use of their WBC's resulted in 93 pregnancies and 114 cases of V.D.

Where the Polish scientists had apparently erred was in their decision to leave the crotch area of their WBC uncovered, to facilitate going to the men's room without the user's having to struggle out of and then back into the WBC. Once they discovered this chink in their armor, it was, as they say in Krakow, back to the old *drawingboardski*.

England was the next to have a go at the WBC. Having sealed off what they referred to as "the Polish corridor," the British investigators sheathed two rugby squads in half-inch thick WBC'S to test the product's tensile strength and the user's ability to perceive sensation.

At the sound of a whistle, the two fifteen-man teams charged one another from opposite ends of a playing field in Eton. On impact, the two rugged rubber rugger teams bounced off one another with such velocity that they hardly felt a thing. Rebounding in all directions, the volunteers, as the scientists duly reported, "were quickly lost to follow-up."

The Germans have employed centuries-old techniques used in stuffing bratwurst to produce a reliable WBC. Composed of a silvery latex casing, the Gummibrat held up admirably in initial testing. Some users reported a tendency to accelerate suddenly while backing up, but after a factory recall, this problem has apparently been rectified. The Gummibrat is available as a single unit or in stringed "links" that can accommodate orgies of up to ten consenting adults.

Once again, the Japanese have shown their genius at miniaturization in their version of the WBC, called the Mini-Con. On removal from its foil wrapper, the Mini-Con resembles a tiny rubber glove with an eccentrically placed thumb.

At a media demonstration held in the auditorium of a Tokyo hotel, a 320-pound Sumo champion managed to wrestle himself into a Mini-Con, pose briefly for photographers, then stride with a squeaking waddle offstage. From behind the curtain emanated a sudden, ear-splitting "POP!" followed by a prolonged, guttural groan.

Meanwhile, the sexually active American male, in the face of terrifying risks of acquiring ghastly diseases, finally achieved what feminists had demanded of him for almost a decade: vulnerability. His bulky sets of condoms, surgical gloves, and mouth dams sorely taxed his libido and that of his partner. Fed up with this piecemeal protection, he tossed the whole kit and caboodle into the wastebasket.

Opening his sock and handkerchief drawer, he extracts a foil-wrapped Mini-Con which a colleague, just returned from Japan, has been kind enough to sell him for an arm and a leg, plus another arm and a leg, and a dingus. It takes him over half an hour to struggle into his Japanese WBC, but he and his female companion are elated with his streamlined look. Until he turns around and she sees the tiny limp tail dangling from his toosh, indicating that he has put his WBC on backwards.

He and his paramour throw on their clothes and go out for hamburgers.

14 WILL FRONTAL NUDITY DESTROY PUBLIC TELEVISION?

*A*CCORDING to the latest issue of *Pornography Alert*, a bulletin published by the Sun Desert retirement community in Palm Springs, the number of sightings of Frontal Nudity on public television increased alarmingly last month.

The publication lists 23 "confirmed" sightings, 47 "possible" sightings and 112 "false" sightings. In the spirit of the Audubon Society, the editors of *Pornography Alert* take pains to authenticate each reported sighting.

According to executive editor Lionel Merkins, "We here at *PA* don't want the issue of Frontal Nudity to meet the same fate as the Unidentified Flying Object. We will not abide the hallucinations of crackpots, the falsified evidence of yellow journalists or the wishful thinking of failed romantics. No, we want Frontal Nudity clearly and unequivocally documented, wherever it may surface, so that we can really sink our teeth into it."

When asked to define Frontal Nudity, Merkins replied, "Frontal, as opposed, say, to Tangential Nudity is quite simply the unclad human body, preferably, for the sake of argument, female, viewed from the front. You can always claim that Tangential Nudity is not pornographic since the inciteful areas of the anatomy are turned away from the viewer. But who can deny that Frontal Nudity, wherein both collar bones and kneecaps are visible, serves any purpose but to inspire lust?"

In its lead editorial this month, *PA* takes PBS to task for being "the largest showcase of Frontal Nudity on American television today." Entitled, "No Wonder They Call it the Boob Tube," the editorial singles out programs on which sightings of Frontal Nudity have been definitely confirmed. They include *The Ascent of Man* (shot of nude model posing for artist), *Monty Python's Flying Circus* (reclining nude in introductory animation), Lord Kenneth Clark's *Romantic Rebellion* (shot of Goya's "Naked Maja"), the Alwin Nikolais Dancers doing "The Relay" and Valerie Perrine glimpsed *flagrante delicto* in Hollywood Television Theater's *Steambath*.

"Possible" sightings have repeatedly occurred during William F. Buckley, Jr.'s *Firing Line*. Thorough investigation by *PA* reporters have revealed that from time to time Mr. Buckley utters a remark so devastating to his guest that the latter, although remaining dressed, gives every appearance of having been stripped completely bare.

Verified "false" sightings have been recorded on *Play Bridge With Experts* and *Wall Street Week*. Last month, a close-up shot of one of the bridge players' hands seemed to reveal that the King of Hearts was naked as a jaybird when, in reality, the nude thumb of the player, covering the King from the neck down and sporting a hangnail, merely gave the illusion of a face card playing the lead in "The Emperor's New Clothes."

As for *Wall Street Week*, a guest stockbroker recently confessed that he had "lost his shirt" last October and was having to "tighten his belt a few notches." An elderly Sun Desert viewer, who later underwent successful cataract surgery, swore she saw a stockbroker naked to the waist begin to fumble with his belt buckle before she was able to click off her set.

Despite these patently false sightings, the executive editor of *PA* is furious with PBS. "Under the cloak of Education and Art lurks the specter of Frontal Nudity," warns Merkins. "Frontal Nudity is but the tip of the pornographic iceberg. The survival of our nation depends on every citizen's ability to stand up, fully clothed, and be counted. Our Pilgrim fathers' simple belief in the virtue of covering up has been a tradition carried forward to modern times. Even in his darkest hours, was Richard Nixon, for example, ever seen on television in less than a suit, shirt, and tie? Shame on you, PBS!"

15 MARRIAGE OF THE MINIMALISTS

SHE created a sensation in New York with her first novel, consisting of a blank cover and 200 empty pages ($18.95 cloth; $7.95 paper). He, on the other hand, was the toast of San Francisco following his one-man show of 65 blank, unsigned and unframed canvases which sold out at an average price of $14.00 per square inch.

They met on *Good Morning America* where they were scheduled to appear conjointly for twelve seconds to comment, as time would allow, on their work. While waiting in the green room to go on TV, the artist glanced at the novelist's cute little button of a nose. He then stared raptly at the wall, finding its uniformly green surface pleasingly complex in its opaqueness but oppressively "painterly" in its colorism.

She caught a glimpse of the cue card he was holding. It directed him to say, "Hi," after the host's introduction. Closing her eyes, she cringed at the necessity imposed by the media for him to say *anything* when his blank canvases said it *all*. With his staring at the wall, and her closing her eyes, it was love at first slight.

When they appeared on camera, the host confessed that he hadn't read her book or had a chance to see his paintings, but was "very happy to welcome both of you, nevertheless, to *Good Morning America*." When the host held up her book and later, when he had the camera focus on one of his paintings, the television screen went blank in 30 million American households, creating a mass defection to *The Today Show*.

After their appearance on *Good Morning America*, he gestured her out to breakfast. With a blank stare, she accepted. She had a demitasse of decaf without cream or sugar and, in unwitting homage to Braque, he had a cube of sugar. He took out his pen and made as if to draw a heart on her napkin; she borrowed his pen and almost wrote "I love you" on *his* napkin, but thought better of it.

They asked the waiter for separate checks. Her demitasse of decaf came to $4.50; his cube of sugar, only $1.25. They both handed the waiter their credit cards. When the multi-layered checks arrived, the minimalist writer refused to sign her name, let alone write in a tip. The minimalist painter carefully extracted the carbon copies from his check, and methodically tore the Customer's Copy, the Merchant's Copy, and the Bank Copy to shreds. The waiter's protests were met with a shower of white and yellow confetti.

They were ordered by the manager to wash dishes for two hours, but they demanded minimum wages. They spent their first night together in adjoining cells at a minimum-security prison. While he demonstrated the sound of one nostril snoring, she vaguely contemplated writing a wordless catalogue for his forthcoming retrospective of paint-free canvases. The next morning the judge pronounced them Guilty as Charged and, as an afterthought, Man and Wife. Overnight, the writer of perfectly limpid prose and the painter of totally uncluttered landscapes had concluded that they were a match made in minimalist heaven, since they both had *nothing* in common.

They pondered briefly where they could spend a minimal honeymoon and chose Des Moines, Iowa. The only physical contact they made on their wedding night was an accidental brushing of elbows as they entered the coffee shop of the Greenfield Motel.

Nine months later she was rushed to the hospital with a swollen elbow. She tried to ignore the whole thing but the doctor insisted on naming it Bursitis. The husband rushed to her bedside, took one look at Bursitis and disclaimed any responsibility. In the end, a judge examined the elbow and awarded the couple joint custody.

Shortly thereafter, they went their separate and indistinct ways. She began turning out slender volumes of totally blank verse and he, taking scissors to canvas, spent the rest of his career as an increasingly minimal miniaturist.

16 STROLLING THE DECK OF CZARS

WE have stepped onto a broad, sun-washed deck in Tiburon. Small, round tables, crowned with dazzling silver and crystal, are spaced at discreet, very expensive intervals. At each table sits a paunchy, balding, middle-aged man and a trim, young blonde woman. Your worst suspicions are about to be confirmed.

Who are these men and women sipping drinks on a sun-washed deck at eleven o'clock on a Thursday morning while the rest of the world is working?

They are, in fact, today's Czars of Industry and their radiant paramours. If you can stand the glare, look at these couples! The sunlight glancing off those portions of the Czars' scalps not sufficiently covered by careful combing is no less intense than that streaming off the hand-waxed bonnets of their Bentleys in the parking lot.

Who are these Czars, with their blondes and their Bentleys, who have earned their place in the sun? For one thing, they are *not* Sheiks, with their redheads and their Rollses, who were *born* with a place in the sun, plus another in the snow at Gstaad. (The Czars would be the first—and the Sheiks the last—to concede that you can't have *everything*.)

Allow me to introduce you to some of these Czars and their stunning companions.

At the most desirable table—against the center of the railing, with an unparalleled view of the Bay and the San Francisco skyline—sits Harry, the Sweat Band Czar. (Net earnings from sales of his designer head bands last year: in excess of 300 million dollars, with plans next month to open his fourth sweat shop in Taipei.) Seated opposite him is Debbie, up from L.A.

Let us eavesdrop at the table of the Sweat Band Czar. Debbie looks up from her Tequila Sunrise and beams Harry a 40,000-watt smile.

"Darling," she asks, "did you fire the upstairs maid yet?"

"Which one?"

"Helga."

"Yeah, I gave Helga her notice last week."

"How much notice?"

"Six years."

Debbie, up from L.A., leans across the table and shoves Harry off the edge of the deck, through the railing and into the Bay. Full of corn chips and guacamole dip, he sinks like a stone—another victim, as the Spanish would say, of "the rapture of the dip."

Harry's sweat band floats to the surface, providing a forlorn marker for the coast guard launch that pulls alongside the deck. During the frenzied rescue efforts, we turn our attention to Roger, the Whoopee Cushion Czar, and Linda, his blonde bombshell, at the next table.

"There goes old Harry again," observes the Whoopee Cushion Czar, making no effort to conceal his glee.

"You think they'll save him this time?" asks Linda.

"I hope not. I've been after Harry's table for three years."

Seated to the right of the Whoopee Cushion Czar is Bradley, the Cat Litter Czar, and Imogene, his pussycat. Despite his efforts to stifle his cough, it is obvious that Bradley suffers from litter lung. Sometimes, as we observe, being a Czar can be hazardous to your health. And your hair style.

Behold—a sudden westerly is creating mass panic among all men on board. The wind is wreaking havoc on their artful arrangement of what little hair they have left on their heads. May Day! May Day!

The moderately balding Mega-Buccaneers lunge for their Ace combs. Desperately, they try to realign the direction of their various wind-blown swoops: starboard to port, port to starboard and most tricky of all, stern to bow. S.O.S.! Save Our Swoops!

All men on board panic, that is, with one exception: Ralph, the Hair Mousse Czar, who sits unruffled through the westerly, each meager strand of his coiffure firmly soldered in place. Not oblivious to the agony of his fellow Czars, he winks smugly across the table at Gigi, his frizzy-headed sweetheart.

Let's drop by and say hello to Marvin, the "Baby-on-Board"

Decal Czar, and Lulu, his nymphet—but you look thirsty! Why don't we sit down at this nice table and have a drink?

Permit me to introduce myself: I am Oscar, the Deck Czar. Can I perhaps interest you in a limited partnership in a lovely platform I'm building in Monaco?

⌐◯ 17 AN EMBARRASSMENT OF BLONDES

*I*N the spring of '83, I rented a Cadillac stretch limo in San Francisco, filled it with unleaded Supreme, seven blondes, fourteen original screenplays, seventy tubes of Topal toothpaste, three dozen bottles of Pert Shampoo for Oily Hair, a liter of Jovan Musk Oil for Men, and instructed the chauffeur to take Highway 5 to Los Angeles.

Below my gray Porsche sunglasses, I wore an 18-carat gold chain around my neck, a beige Sulka shirt, light wool slacks the color of Bud's French Vanilla ice cream, and tan Gucci loafers. I was hoping to sell a screenplay or two and didn't want to look like an *Ausländer*.

As we approached Sunset Boulevard, my chauffeur pulled into the Arriving Limo Lane. He stopped at the Immigration Checkpoint where two of my blondes were detained for interrogation and three of my screenplays were shredded. A uniformed guard patiently explained,

"Sir, we've got a major blonde glut here. Like the natives are starting to call Westwood 'Little Oslo.' The Screen Actors' Guild has set the quota—no more than five blondes to a limo."

"Whoa!" I said. "Wait till the A.C.L.U. hears about this! Through an accident of birth, these women may be blondes—or may not—but they are thinking, feeling human beings. I may have brought them here for protective coloration, but I cherish them as friends. And why have you shredded three of my screenplays?"

"The first was derivative," said the guard, "and the character of the female lead was two-dimensional. The second script would have required a budget of 30 mil just for the special effects. The third was effete, lamely poetic, and had the visual impact of oatmeal."

"But . . . but," I sputtered, "who are *you* to judge?"

"All my buddies and I here at the Checkpoint are graduates of the USC Film School. Four years on the campus gave us a *pretty* good eye for ersatz blondes and crummy screenplays."

Saluting smartly, he waved the rest of us on through. I quickly calculated that I still had five blondes and eleven screenplays and all my other trinkets. As I ordered the chauffeur to head for the Beverly Hills Hotel, I concluded that my losses at the Checkpoint were not only acceptable and a valuable learning experience, but had left me leaner and meaner. (The man who said seven blondes could live as cheaply as five was a dreamer.)

After I slipped the maître d' of the Polo Lounge a mint-crisp hundred-dollar bill, he ordered a busboy to clear a table for five.

"But there are six of us."

"I'm sorry, sir, but local ordinances limit the number of blondes at one table to four."

I asked one of the young ladies (the only one not named Heather) to wait in the car with the chauffeur. I slipped the maître d' another C-note and our party of five was seated at a power table under a jacaranda tree in full blossom. I was beginning to enjoy myself. A waiter took our order for drinks and had some nice things to say about one of my scripts.

I glanced around at the other tables where svelte, expensively tailored men and women were animatedly talking about rolling grosses, final cuts, and foreign rights.

"I'm glad you like my script," I told the waiter. "Tell me—is there anyone around here you might suggest I show it to?"

The waiter summoned a busboy who, after introducing himself as Martin, poured us each a glass of ice water. The waiter handed him my screenplay and said, "Martin, this gentleman would like some input from you on this script."

When Martin left with his water jug and my screenplay, I said to the waiter, "But this is an insult. I came all the way down here from San Francisco to sell a movie script and it winds up in the hands of a busboy!"

"Oh, but you don't understand, sir. If Martin likes your script, he'll deliver it with the rolls and butter to Mr. Gottlieb seated behind you and if *he* likes it, you're in."

I turned around and there, surrounded by four Bo Derek-class blondes, was the only man over sixty in Hollywood who could afford to let himself grow fat and bald: Sidney I. Gottlieb, the legendary producer. My four generic blondes fled to the ladies' room for emergency repairs, but not before smiling winsomely at Mr. Gottlieb.

When we finished our dessert and coffee, Mr. Gottlieb not only insisted on picking up my tab, but had me sign a six-figure contract for my screenplay. Not bad for my first afternoon in Hollywood.

A year later, the movie made from my script lost $57 million for Sidney I. Gottlieb's studio. Undaunted, I returned to the Polo Lounge with my slightly frayed screenplays and somewhat frazzled blondes.

To my dismay, the waiter pointedly ignored my scripts while he recited the specials of the day. My spirits revived when a gaunt busboy with an ill-fitting, dark-brown toupee plucked the top script off my stack and said, "I think the group at Mr. Spielberg's table will appreciate this one."

The busboy walked over to Steven Spielberg's table, bent down and wedged my script under one of the table legs, thereby curing an annoying wobble.

The busboy returned to my side and announced, "Mr. Spielberg sends his compliments. Can I get you some more rolls, Dr. London?"

"No thank you, Sidney," I said. "Oh by the way, aren't those your old blondes being seated at the Perlmutter table?"

Headache Remedies

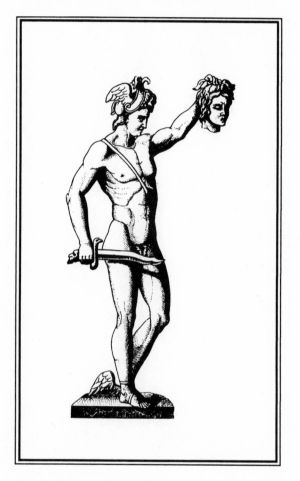

18 NEW HOPE FOR THE *SUNDAY TIMES* JUNKIE

*U*NTIL recent years, the addictive properties of the *Sunday New York Times* were largely an insular problem. Now that its subscribers have become as far-flung from the island of Manhattan as its correspondents, the *Sunday Times*, it is feared, will soon find itself on a list of Controlled Substances.

By now, every large city in the nation has been the scene of a major *Sunday Times* bust. On the front pages of local newspapers an all-too familiar headline, "80 Pounds of *Sunday Times* Seized in Suburban Apartment," appears over the hackneyed photo of an obscenely bulging plastic bag lying atop a heavily guarded breakfast table.

It would be hard to spot the typical *Sunday Times* junkie in, say, a crowd of businessmen waiting to board a commuter train in Denver. Six days out of seven, he is indistinguishable from his fellow Westerners except for a tad less padding in the shoulders of his suit and perhaps a tendency to use the word "clearly" a bit more than is absolutely necessary.

He lies in his bed at four A.M. on Sunday morning, staring at the ceiling. The pupils of his eyes are dilated to their outer limits by a week of *Sunday Times* withdrawal. Involuntarily, he begins to moisten the tip of his right index finger and methodically turn phantom pages. Suddenly, at ten of five, a joyous THUMP resounds in his driveway.

His neck veins bulge from the weight of the imperfectly rain-proofed package in his arms. He locks himself up in his study and tremulously spreads out a fathomless sea of newsprint on the floor. Like a snorkler clamping on goggles, he affixes his reading glasses and surrenders himself to the rapture of the deep-think piece.

By three in the afternoon, he has missed both church and the football game, and his children are threatening to turn him in to the Sheriff's Office. He couldn't care less. Like a fly in amber, he's entombed inside *The Week in Review*. And he hasn't even cracked *Business* yet, not to mention *Arts & Leisure, Obituaries,* and *Real Estate*.

Just after eleven o'clock on Sunday night, his wife manages to persuade him, at the top of her lungs, to phone the *Sunday Times* Hot Line. Still reading voraciously, with no end in sight, and not a bite to eat for eighteen hours, he is almost grateful to her for suggesting there might be a way out of the *Sunday Times*. With the ink-stained tip of his right index finger, he dials a toll-free number:

VOLUNTEER: (*cultured, middle-aged female voice*) Thank you for calling the *Sunday Times* Hot Line—may I assist you?

ADDICT: Uh, not really. Hey, look, I'm not one of those guys who've got to have their *Times* fix every day. I just fool around with it a little bit on weekends.

VOLUNTEER: Of course. In what section are you now?

ADDICT: *Music*. A piece by Will Crutchfield on the long-awaited opening of the Toscanini family archives. Fascinating stuff. . . . Oh, God! Please help! GET ME OUT OF HERE!

VOLUNTEER: So—now we can begin. What, may I ask, is your first name?

ADDICT: Fred.

VOLUNTEER: Okay, Fred. Pay attention—the only way you're going to extricate yourself from the *Sunday Times* is to *retrace your every step*. If you try to break out by continuing to read, you'll never make it.

ADDICT: But I haven't even started the crossword puzzle yet.

VOLUNTEER: Listen to me carefully, Fred. We're not here on 24-hour alert to give you a five-letter word for the bow of Vishnu. Once you're trapped inside those little boxes in the puzzle, the only escape is by rioting, which we are not authorized to condone, foment or suppress.

ADDICT: Can't I just skim over *Food, Books,* and *Travel* before you take over?

VOLUNTEER: *Food, Books,* and *Travel* are known as "The Bermuda Triangle" around here. Fred, close your eyes and listen. I'm going to walk you back through your discarded pages. Stay with me and you'll emerge a free man. Otherwise, in the morning, you'll be a dead fish wrapped in yesterday's newspaper. What did you read before that piece on the Toscanini archives?

ADDICT: Russell Baker.

VOLUNTEER: (*quickly finding the page*) Got it—Baker. Yes, well, (*unable to control herself*) ha. He's *very* good today, isn't he? Fred, where were you before Baker?

ADDICT: *Real Estate.* Something about sellers finding condo resales shaky.

VOLUNTEER: (*pauses to enter data in her PC*) Fred, here's what you do: Start with Crutchfield on Toscanini— read only the first line of each paragraph. Then glance at the headline on that condo piece and run through the scores of last week's baseball games. Finally, riffle *backwards* through the pages of *Week in Review* and you're home free!

ADDICT: (*Silence*)

VOLUNTEER: Fred? . . . Fred? Are you there? Fred!

ADDICT: Look, there's a terrific piece here on "The Unromantic Generation." Can I get back to you in a couple of hours?

The inherent limitations of the *Sunday Times* Hot Line have led to the setting up of regional debriefing centers. On admission, an addict is assigned a private room and forty kilos of an uncut *Sunday Times.* Each successive week, one section is withdrawn.

After nine weeks, the addict is administered a British publication entitled, *Cricket This Week.* To date, no *Sunday Times* addict has survived more than the first three pages of *Cricket This Week* without begging to be released to the custody of his family.

Once again, the ex-*Sunday Times* junkie stands in line waiting at day's end for the 5:12. He smiles condescendingly at his fellow businessmen burying their noses in *The Wall Street Journal.*

"Clearly, what these men are doing is *snorting* the closing averages," he observes, straightening his shoulders beneath their slightly attenuated pads.

19 FOR EACH EPOCH ITS OWN POISON

*W*an in Rome: Lead poisoning did more to hasten the decline and fall of the Roman Empire than did the Visigoths and Vandals. Archaeological evidence clearly indicates that the Roman aristocracy was slowly poisoned by leaden pipes and receptacles used in the better homes and gardens of the Empire. Biochemists have confirmed that the effluent of the affluent contained neurologically toxic doses of lead. In a sense, Rome was destroyed by a sort of reverse alchemy: On receipt of history's first outrageous plumbing bill, Romans saw their gold transformed into lead.

Like Rome, other cultures have succumbed to chemical toxicity. In the Paris of the Twenties, Gertrude Stein's Lost Generation discovered that absinthe not only made the heart grow fonder but served as an effective embalming fluid. While the poets of Ireland drowned in 90-proof whiskey in the pubs of Dublin, the creative lights of Vienna were burning out on caffeine in the coffeehouses of the Ringstrasse.

Caffeine und Vien: Fin de siècle Vienna was home to a brilliant group of writers, artists, composers, architects, and psychoanalysts, each of whom was ultimately incapacitated by an overdose of caffeine. In the famous coffeehouses of the Ringstrasse the intelligentsia got their lumps.

Slurping *Kaffee mit Schlagg* from seven in the morning till three the *next* morning, they went back to their garrets bright-eyed and bushy-tailed. In a frenzy of coffee nerves, they couldn't sleep. So they wrote, painted, composed—anything to keep busy. Then, pale and still shaking, they scurried back to the coffeehouses for their 7 A.M. fix.

Small wonder the bright flame of creativity in *fin de siècle* Vienna fizzled out so quickly! Under the influence of caffeine, the Viennese intelligentsia talked themselves to death!

After the third cup of the new day, coffeehouse patrons had a tendency to override their table-partner's conversation. After the fifth cup, they were at each other's throats.

For example, observe Freud, between patients, sitting down with Mahler, between symphonies, for a cup of coffee. They exchange formal pleasantries, light up cigars, and guzzle their brew for a spell.

"So, my dear Gustav, (*slurp*) how's your Third Symphony coming along?" Freud finally asks.

"Sigmund, my friend, (*slurp*) don't ask," says Mahler. "In the second movement, I'm having the deuce of a time trying to decide how many violas I need to—"

"*Ach*, an artistic block!" cries the doctor, emptying his cup with a Freudian slurp and whipping out his notebook. "And, so, did your childhood fixation on the viola-shaped body of your mother dominate your every—"

"What are you (*slurp*) ranting about, Sigmund? If my mother were built like a *bassoon*—which she wasn't!—what business of *yours* would it—"

Freud pushes his chair back from the table, and leaps to his feet.

"Waiter!" he shouts, "Herr Mahler wishes the bill! Call me a couch! I mean a coach!" (Something is gained here in translation.)

Freud storms out of the coffeehouse while, at adjoining tables, Schönberg is shouting atonally at Wittgenstein, Arthur Schnitzler is throttling Karl Kraus, and Klimt is kicking Kokoschka in the shins.

From Reefers to Reagan: It is highly likely that marijuana was the undoing of the Beat Generation of the Fifties, just as LSD, disguised as a love potion, did in the Hippies of the Sixties. After the Best and the Brightest of America went up in smoke or dissolved in acid, we were left with the Modest and the Mediocre, who comprised the Me Decade.

Working hard, jogging hard, breeding little, they wisely squirreled away a sizable portion of their double-incomes against the day they knew they'd have to enter a cocaine detox center. (If you think the street price of cocaine is inflated, check out those private clinic fees!) So after the best and the brightest self-destructed, and the wispy dreams of the modest and the mediocre disappeared up their nostrils, the country was left in the hands of the worst and the dumbest.

In the Eighties, we faced the pernicious influence of lite beer on Reagan's America. Due to the insipid ingredients of this libation, it took six years for the blood alcohol levels of Reagan's advisers to reach the critical levels that finally precipitated such misadventures as arms for hostages and the CIA drug connection. America, as they say, gets the leaders it deserves. Let there be Lite.

20 BJÖRN LOSER'S FINAL REJECTION

*T*HE nation's freelance writers mourned the sudden passing last winter of San Francisco author, Björn Loser. In a literary career that spanned five decades, Loser had the distinction of being the most prolific unpublished writer in the Western Hemisphere. His loss meant that no longer could a rejected freelance writer take comfort in the thought that at least poor old Loser had been rejected that week as well.

For months after his demise, rejection slips poured into Loser's mailbox from editors he had sent manuscripts to during his final weeks. He thus became that literary rarity: a posthumously rejected author.

His wife and executor, Mrs. Ima Loser, donated his vast collection of rejection slips and unpublished manuscripts to the Bay Area Recycling Center which promptly returned them to her with a short, computer-generated note stating that the overworked staff at BARC regretted that it did not have time to respond personally to every submission but wanted to thank her nevertheless for thinking of BARC.

Loser's memorial service at the City Lights Bookstore was attended by legions of stricken friends, loving family members, and guilty editors from all corners of the English-speaking world. Several editors were asked to speak at the service. A sampling of their heart-felt comments follows:

> "He never failed to enclose a self-addressed stamped envelope." (*The Atlantic Monthly*)
> "We were always favorably impressed with the generosity of his margins." (*The New Yorker*)

"With the possible exceptions of Henry James and William Faulkner, we have never come across a writer who punctuated so beautifully." (*Harper's Magazine*)

"When Loser declared that there were, say, about 2000 words in the manuscript, you could be sure there were, indeed, about 2000 words in the manuscript. He could count circles around Hemingway." (*The Paris Review*)

"Most authors indent their paragraphs five spaces; Loser boldly indented his eight spaces. Whenever we'd see a manuscript with an eight-space indentation, we'd say, "Another Loser!" and stuff it into the return envelope." (*Field & Stream*)

"Loser was not without a sense of humor. He once sent us back a rejection slip with the comment, 'The enclosed material does not suit my needs at this time.'" (*Esquire*)

Loser's six-page Last Will and Testament was successfully contested by his brother, Thor, a novelist manqué. To add insult to injury, Thor Loser stood up at the memorial service and announced that he refused to read Björn's "Parting Words to My Family and Friends" on grounds that they were hackneyed, single-spaced and had not been preceded by a query.

21 WAS ANNE BOLEYN JUST ANOTHER FACE ON THE CUTTING ROOM FLOOR?

*T*HE risks of general anesthesia can be so horrific that doctors are forever searching for new ways to eliminate pain during surgery.

In a few avant-garde hospitals in San Francisco, slightly doctored videotapes are replacing general anesthesia as a means of inducing coma in preoperative patients. Painstakingly edited by a dozen caffeine addicts in a Berkeley studio, the video tapes have been culled from contemporary TV programs.

Patients who wish their gall bladders painlessly removed without the risks of conventional anesthesia may elect to view the following tape:

UNINTERRUPTED PLEDGE BREAKS. Devoid of stimulating intrusions by *Masterpiece Theater* or *Great Performances*, this eight-hour cassette of public television pledge breaks features non-stop monologues by silver-tongued bearers of tin cups. Between trembling close-ups of Edith Piaf album covers, the camera pans over banks of drowsy operators, each sprouting a beige phone, like a goiter, in the crook of the neck.

The sight, but not sound, of thirty telephone conversations in progress is usually sufficient for the anesthesiologist to signal to the surgeon that the patient is ready. For the next ninety minutes, the patient dreams that he is donating his gall bladder to public television.

The patient's glazed eyes remain open during the entire operation. If the anesthesiologist detects signs that the tape is losing its effect, he ejects UNINTERRUPTED PLEDGE BREAKS and inserts PITCHER THROWS TO FIRST. The producers of the latter tape have pieced together two hours of major league pitchers of various stripes and spitting styles, wheeling on the mound and throwing the ball to first base. The patient begins to moan.

The anesthesiologist then inserts SATELLITE PICTURES OF THE CENTRAL STATES quickly followed by APPROACH SHOTS TO THE 14TH GREEN. As a last resort, he administers THE COMPLETE RECITATIVES FROM THE RING CYCLE. The patient gratefully relapses into coma.

22 FOUR & TWENTY BLACKBIRDS TAPED ON THE SLY

*N*OVA, that venerable science program, recently addressed itself to the question, "Why Do Birds Sing?" The ornithologists on NOVA were quick to point out that, aside from an occasional wolf-whistle by a male bird to attract a mate, birds primarily sing in order to map out territorial boundaries. In a given plot of woodland or field, each species negotiates at the top of its lungs for a piece of *lebensraum.*

Myriads of overlapping subdivisions are formed when birds of a different feather move into the same neighborhood. As I saw it on NOVA, Mother Nature, in her intuitive wisdom, devised this complexity of closely guarded, interlocking nesting grounds for the proliferation of the species and Ph.D. theses. Turn a flock of doctoral candidates loose in a meadow and watch the feathers fly!

To tell the truth, I was taken aback by some of the scientific methods described on NOVA to probe the hidden meanings of birdsong. I refer to the secret installation of recording devices beneath unwary chirpers. This bugging of birdnests smacked a bit too much of Watergate for my comfort. We can thank the producers of NOVA for making these shocking tapes a matter of public record.

In another experiment, scientists tampered with the recording of a redwing blackbird's song in an effort to make it sound ugly. Even played at one-fourth speed, the call was a hauntingly beautiful thrum. Ah! But how would a bird sound if its syrinx were partially paralyzed? With its vocal organ weakened, surely the bird would sound ghastly. And then—cameras ready!—wouldn't its fine feathered friends turn their backs on him?

After performing an exceedingly delicate operation in which one of the nerves to the syrinx of a volunteer bird was severed, the scientists triumphed again. The postoperative cry of the mutilated blackbird, dutifully recorded on an oscillograph, was just about the saddest song I've ever heard. Indeed, the other blackbirds appeared to share my revulsion when the released bird attempted to tell his friends about his operation.

In another experiment, scientists inked out the scarlet markings on a red-winged blackbird in order to observe whether his peers would still recognize him. When this all-black bird was insinuated back into its neighborhood, his red-winged brothers picked up and fled to the suburbs. This clearly bigoted response indicated that the investigators had unwittingly created a new avian species: the red-necked blackbird.

What the ornithologists proceeded to do with their pirated recordings of birdsong was equally disgraceful. Toting a gigantic loudspeaker, they sneaked into the nesting ground of a red-winged blackbird. Without so much as the courtesy of announcing, "The following is a recorded message," they began to play back the shrill call of a rival blackbird. Hoodwinked by this high-fidelity scam, the bird swooped down from its family tree and perched militantly on the brim of the shrieking loud-speaker. In unmistakable body language, the bird dropped more than a hint of its outrage at this patent violation of the Bill of Rights. (Some may argue that a bird has no rights, but who, I ask, can deny that a bird has a bill?)

My final assessment of "Why Do Birds Sing?" was that it posed a question more fittingly addressed to poets than scientists. Keats, for example, fielded it rather well, I think, when he answered,

That thou, light-winged Dryad of the trees,
In some melodious plot
Of beechen green, and shadows numberless,
Singest of summer in full-throated ease.

23 THANK GOD FOR MEDI-CAR

*M*Y German luxury sedan is, as they say in Bavaria, on the fritz. A minor setback, I am told, having to do with the fuel injector, the microprocessor and the transmission. Am I worried? *Nein. Ich habe . . .* that is, I have a five-year, 50,000-mile warranty.

What is more, my policy states that in the event of my own demise before the expiration of the warranty, my heirs shall be entitled to 3% financing on a new car of the same make in perpetuity—plus fleet rates on car rentals for the funeral. I mean, if my car and I get totaled in an intersection, how pretty can I sit?

My ailing German vehicle has been in a Convalescent Repair Shop for the past five months. The concept of the C.R.S. is a phenomenon of the Eighties—a decade which brought into confluence the unreliability of computer-intensive cars and the what's-the-hurry time-frame of extended warranties.

It was not easy getting my elderly '81 sedan into the Edelweiss Convalescent Repair Shop. The waiting list was a mile long and four cars wide. Located in the metallic-gray area between San Francisco and Daly City, the Edelweiss has a reputation for providing disabled German vehicles with an ideal ambience for maximum recovery of insured parts (EXCLUSIVE OF CERTAIN POWERTRAIN COMPONENTS AND EMISSION CONTROL SYSTEMS).

Before I could get my car into the Edelweiss, it was necessary for me to donate $500 to The Friends of the Edelweiss Convalescent Repair Shop—a non-profit organization with offices in Palm Springs, Newport Beach, and Beverly Hills.

I can't remember getting a happier phone call in my life than the one from the Edelweiss instructing me to have my car towed to their admitting office. (For three weeks it had lingered near death in my driveway.)

In the spotless lobby of the Edelweiss, Herr Wächter, director of the Convalescent Repair Shop, greeted me warmly. After examining my car, he ordered its precious bodily fluids drained and replaced with fresh infusions of 10-40 motor oil, distilled water, and premium unleaded gas. He himself hooked the carburetor to a pacemaker, cleaned the windshield, and checked the tires.

Talk about intensive care! This guy was terrific!

As Herr Wächter led me to a spiffy German compact (rented from Edelweiss Leasing), I knew that my enfeebled family car was in good hands.

I'm allowed to spend time with my vehicle each day during visiting hours. The first three months were the toughest. The mechanics ran every diagnostic test in the factory manual and couldn't figure out what was wrong.

The flowers I sent—a huge bouquet of garagiolas—seemed, at first, to do the trick.

My sedan rallied sufficiently in the next week to permit me, accompanied by a male nurse in white overalls, to drive it around the block at no more than ten miles per hour, twice daily. Lately, I've been allowed to take it on short trips to the country.

Although it's lost a lot of its former pizazz, my car is definitely on the mend. Herr Wächter says he is confident that I can look forward to full recovery by the fifteenth of January—oddly enough, the same date the warranty runs out.

24 FJORDSTROM LOVES ME

*F*JORDSTROM Department Stores are justly famous for their intensely personal service. It is almost impossible to buy anything more expensive than a handkerchief at Fjordstrom without getting a cordial letter from the salesperson a few days later. Until I was apprehended last month in the men's department, pocketing eight pairs of gloves, I would never have guessed that Fjordstrom's legendary solicitousness extended to shoplifters.

I must confess to suffering from kleptomania. I've seen a dozen psychiatrists in the past decade about this problem and have ended up with three leather couches, 144 issues of *National Geographic*, and twelve beautifully framed diplomas. In each case, the court found me not guilty by reason of insanity and assigned me to yet another psychiatrist. In a word, I'm incorrigible.

To all appearances, Fjordstrom offers as much challenge to the shoplifter as a miniature golf course to Jack Nicklaus. As I was casually stuffing the eight pairs of gloves into the right-hand pocket of my camel's hair overcoat from Brooks Brothers, the most lovely and eager-to-please salesperson I've ever met came up to me. Ms. Sweetland proceeded to insert three woolen scarves, a bottle of Antaeus cologne, and a dozen silk ties by Oscar de la Renta into my other pocket. I was about to thank her profusely when I found myself surrounded by Fjordstrom's SWAT team. The latter consisted of twenty graduates of divinity school dressed in navy blue blazers and gray slacks—as sweet a bunch of guys armed with Uzis as you'd ever care to meet.

The judge was prepared to free me on my lawyer's customary

plea of insanity, when the magistrate discovered that his gavel was missing. The bailiff body-searched me on the spot and chanced upon the gavel in the breast pocket of my recently acquired Harris tweed jacket. The outraged judge sentenced me to one-to-five years at San Quentin. I had served no more than three days when I received the following letter from Fjordstrom:

13 May 88

Mr. Milton Honeybreath
Assistant Director,
Customer Services
Fjordstrom,
Mill Valley, CA

Dr. Oscar London
Cell 1236-A
San Quentin, CA

Dear Dr. London:

Thank you for shoplifting at Fjordstrom. Our Ms. Sweetland was very favorably impressed with your choice of our Winter-on-the-Moors leather gloves. Made of the finest center-cut, hand-kneaded calfskin, our Winter-on-the-Moors gloves are imported by us from Harrod's in London. I'm sorry you failed to notice that the gloves were marked down 50%—a virtual steal, if you will kindly pardon the expression, at $37.50 the pair. May I suggest that the next time you shoplift at Fjordstrom, you take advantage of our free delivery service? You would then be met by our SWAT team in the comfort of your own home.

May your time fly, Dr. London! In the meantime, please accept, under separate cover, our complimentary pair of Winter-on-the-Moors leather gloves. Guaranteed for five years, they should certainly provide you with some measure of comfort during your morning workouts in the prison yard for at least the maximum duration of your sentence.

Looking forward to the resumption of your patronage on your eventual parole or escape, I remain

Your humble plaintiff,

Milton Honeybreath
Customer Services
Fjordstrom

☐ 25 NEW CURE FOR WRITER'S BLOCK

*R*EUBEN Anthony Fishlowitz, poet (*Synchrony II*), novelist (*No Tootsie for Nussbaum*), and playwright (*Arugula*), was utterly blocked. Febrile of eye, tangled of hair, ample of paunch, the forty-three-year-old author was writing at the top of his form when inexplicably the words stopped coming.

It happened on page 131 of his new novel (untitled). Fishlowitz was blithely tapping out a love scene involving his hero, Dr. Nathan Flank (a neonatal urologist) and Ms. Tanya Tolltaker (a Bay Bridge employee) when the author was seized by a sudden pang of hunger.

With Tanya's heaving bosom securely cupped in Nathan's "powerful, rubber-gloved grip," Fishlowitz clicked "SAVE" on his file menu, rose from his Macintosh, and retired to his kitchenette. After a ten-minute snack of Hot Mexican Cheese Whiz on an egg & onion matzoh, washed down with a diet A & W, he returned to Nathan and Tanya and—nothing.

Despite the insistent hum of his Macintosh and the shrieks of his heroine, Fishlowitz could not write another word. Full of Whiz, fizz, and apprehension, he scanned the previous two pages and was overcome with a sickening suspicion that what he had written so far was drivel. The love affair between the humorless, compulsive Flank and the hot-tempered, powerfully-sexed Tolltaker suddenly seemed to Fishlowitz, for want of a better word, contrived.

After being dolefully stared at for three hours, the Macintosh automatically flashed the message: WRITER'S BLOCK. GO TO BED. Fishlowitz, the darling of the second seating of the literary lunch set at the "Washbag" (Washington Square Bar and Grill), was blocked!

He frantically began calling his friends. Feldman the essayist suggested a thirty-minute power walk followed by a cold shower. Feldman's advice resulted in a shin splint and a mild chill. Blocked! Shapiro the fantasist advised dressing in a bridal gown and standing for an hour on the corner of Market and Fifth. Shapiro's suggestion netted Fishlowitz $13.45 in spare change. Blocked! Seligman the satirist counseled sipping ice water while slowly breathing through the nose—a maneuver that precipitated a 72-hour bout of hiccups. Blocked!

As days turned into weeks and Fishlowitz remained blocked, his friends conceded that their pen pal was in deep trouble and rallied around him. Interrupting their own work, they took turns sitting up with him all night, cajoling him, fluffing his aura, and reassuring him that his block was temporary.

As word of Fishlowitz's block spread among the literati, the Washbag's protocol committee, over the protest of his friends, demoted him to the third seating which consisted of poets manqué and frequently published writers of letters to the editor. Convinced that his friends had sabotaged him, Fishlowitz vowed revenge.

Still loyal, his friends pitched in and sent Fishlowitz on an Amtrak tour to Tijuana in hopes that travel would unblock him—or at least get him out of their hair for a while. His friends slyly gave Fishlowitz self-addressed postcards which he dutifully mailed back. Each recipient found the left side of his postcard accusingly blank.

Fishlowitz returned from Mexico with a bout of turista so violent that his physician reported his case history to the *Annals of Gastroenterology*. "Fishlowitz has turista and he's still blocked!" roared Feldman the essayist during a second seating at the Washbag.

The hapless author not only inspired his doctor to write at length, but his lawyer as well. In an epic brief, Sidney Weintraub, attorney at law, notified Fishlowitz's friends that they were being sued for railroading his client to Mexico and causing him grievous bodily harm.

Pawning their word processors, his stricken friends settled out of court. Rather than his turista, it was Fishlowitz's writer's block that proved contagious. Feldman, Shapiro, and Seligman all became terminally blocked.

Meanwhile, Fishlowitz's handsome settlement had a most

gratifying effect. Miraculously unblocked, Fishlowitz finally freed Tanya Tolltaker from the non-skid clutches of Dr. Flank. In a marathon session, Fishlowitz wrote 200 seamless pages to complete his novel which he triumphantly entitled, *For Whom the Belle Tolls*.

Fishlowitz's novel rapidly rose on the Best Seller lists and he appeared on *The Today Show*. To the agony of his former friends, he was elevated to first seating at the Washbag. As his old buddies schlepped in for the second seating and passed his table, he cut them dead.

One afternoon, after a wildly successful signing at B. Dalton on Kearny, Fishlowitz was picked up by a black stretch limo. Fishlowitz assumed the limo had been provided by his publisher. Rather, it turned out, the limo appeared as the result of his ex-friends having made a non-literary contract with a cement firm loosely affiliated with the Contra Costa Cosa Nostra.

On December 20th of 1979, Reuben Anthony Fishlowitz, poet, novelist, and playwright, suddenly sank out of sight. Last month, during a dredging operation in San Francisco Bay, the good ship *Neamiah* pulled up a huge rectangular slab of concrete. Faintly etched on one side was the label, "Writer's Block."

◼◻ 26 BOMBED AT TAHOE

*U*NTIL elements of the Sixth Fleet were sent into Lake Tahoe to shell hotels and casinos along the South Shore, I had tended to pooh-pooh the influence of the Moral Majority on national policy. I was sitting at a $5 blackjack table inside Harrah's at 4:30 A.M. when the first salvo came in.

A noisy craps table on the far side of the casino took a direct hit on the Come line. I looked up to see croupiers, chips, ashtrays, dice, a green-felt table top and high-rollers all seeming to rise from the floor in slow motion—a floating crap game, to all appearances—before disappearing into a cloud of cigarette and gun smoke.

Figuring that gamblers who die while shooting craps end up as holy rollers in seventh heaven, I returned to my blackjack game. Oblivious to the bombardment, the sleepy-eyed dealer glanced at her watch in anticipation of her next break and asked if I wanted another card.

I had just about decided to stand pat with a sixteen against her two of hearts up-card, when the second salvo hit. The ear-splitting vibes of a rock combo in the lounge were abruptly silenced when an eight-inch shell struck the second guitarist on his 250 watt instrument just below the waistline. (Listen, how can you mourn the break-up of a group that so eagerly invited comparison with the Grateful Dead?)

Along about this time, a few nervous nellies among the customers began cashing in their chips. Refusing to panic, we die-hard gamblers signalled for fresh drinks to the gamely smiling cocktail waitresses—God bless them!—and bet the limit at the craps, roulette and the blackjack tables. We were determined to die with our bets on, as it were.

A half-hour later, with bombs bursting in air, what so proudly we hailed by the dawn's early light was the rocket-red glare of the keno board. The casino had not surrendered! Hip-hip Harrah!

Between explosions, we could still hear the Bingo caller nasally intoning through her microphone, "B . . . 6 . . . N . . . 24 . . . G . . . 52. . . ." When the next shell burst, she asked, "Did I hear a Bingo?" I mean, you gotta admire *sangfroid* like that.

Throughout the bombardment, elderly ladies in immaculate slack suits stood their ground at the slot machines and hung on for dear life. From time to time, flying shrapnel would strike a machine, causing cascades of nickels and cries of "Edith, lookee here!"

Meanwhile, I was beginning to find the whole situation intolerable. Once or twice a year I go up to Tahoe for a little R & R. For this I'm willing to risk five hundred, maybe six hundred bucks. But my life? Deal me out.

I mean, if the Moral Majority wants to get rid of gambling at Tahoe, all it has to do is persuade Congress to make it illegal to split aces and eight's.

After losing fifty bucks on a nineteen to the dealer's twenty, I nodded farewell to the bloody but unbowed pit boss and to the sole surviving table mate on my left, a visiting tire dealer from Medford, Oregon. The Medfordian shifted his position slightly on his stool to avoid a burst of machine gun fire and said, "Last time I come to Tahoe. You don't get as nice a crowd in Reno but it sure as hell's quieter."

I stepped outside just as a dawn patrol of Navy dive bombers wiped out the entire west wall of the Sahara Tahoe Hotel. You can just imagine what was going on inside the rooms in full view of us innocent bystanders. It's truly amazing how people behave when they think they're safe behind locked bedroom doors. And here I thought gambling was the favorite indoor sport at Tahoe!

Picture, if you will, a giant, exposed honeycomb of hundreds of heterosexual couples lying side-by-side in bed, watching the *MacNeil-Lehrer Report*. I will never forget the sight of those countless heads of Robin MacNeil gleaming pink through the smoke-filled dawn at Tahoe. Judging by the small logo over his head, I think he was talking about price supports for Midwestern farmers.

The battle ended abruptly when the neon billboard in front of Caesars Tahoe suddenly flashed, WELCOME SIXTH FLEET! Hey, who can beat the hospitality at Lake Tahoe?

Liniments
(Sports Medicine)

27 THE LOUISVILLE CORKER AND THE MILLION DOLLAR T-SHIRT

*T*HE widespread impounding and X-raying of baseball bats for suspected cork implants is threatening to destroy the national pastime. Scenes like the following are being repeated at radiologists' offices in big-league cities all over the country:

The waiting room of the X-ray department in a major San Francisco hospital. A muscular young man in a baseball uniform sits clutching his bandaged head in both hands. A nurse appears at the door and beckons him.

NURSE: Doctor will see you now.

Young man is ushered into the darkened reading room of Dr. Seymour Rifkin, Radiologist. The only illumination is a sickly gray light passing through a set of X-rays on the viewing box.

DR. RIFKIN: Sit down, Mr. Boscoe. Well, I'm sorry to say I've got some bad news for you.

YOUNG MAN: (*paling*) Oh no, Doc. Not . . .

DR. RIFKIN: I'm afraid so. (*points to an X-ray*) Look—all through the head. Cork. The worst bat scan I've ever seen. I'm going to have to report this to the Commissioner.

YOUNG MAN: Please, Doc. The guy I bought the bat from said it was pure hickory. How was I suppose to know it was corked?

DR. RIFKIN: Your batting average of .412 should have tipped you off. How's your head feeling?

YOUNG MAN: (*groans*). A pitcher thinks I've corked my bat so he beans me with a fast ball between my eyes!

My head's *killing* me, Doc. What do you see on them X-rays of my skull?

DR. RIFKIN: (*points to another film*) Good news, Mr. Boscoe. I don't see any cork. Just pure hickory.

Major leaguers are also flocking to psychiatrists' offices because of the overwhelming guilt caused by their hyperinflated salaries.

The consultation room of Dr. Morris ("Lefty") Tannenbaum, psychoanalyst specializing in emotional disorders of pitchers and centerfielders. The doctor sits at the head of a glove-leather couch on which is stretched the long supine form of an overwrought, overpaid pitcher.

DR. TANNENBAUM: Mr. Graelski, you still haven't told me how much you're pulling down each year.

PITCHER: I cain't, Doc. It's too embarrassin'.

DR. TANNENBAUM: Oh, come on, son. Just give me a ballpark figure.

PITCHER: I jist cain't.

DR. TANNENBAUM: Is it more than $100,000?

PITCHER: (*deeply affronted*) Of course I makes more'n that! What do you thank I am—a *bat boy?*

DR. TANNENBAUM: Certainly not, Mr. Graelski. I simply want to know your salary in order to explore with you the psychiatric implications.

PITCHER: Say what?

DR. TANNENBAUM: Your win-loss record so far this year is four and eleven. This must cause you considerable guilt and anxiety. It means you're being paid a small fortune to lose more ballgames than you win.

PITCHER: (*whimpers*) Have a heart, Doc.

DR. TANNENBAUM: So what's your income?

PITCHER: (*taking a deep breath*) You want salary—or salary plus residuals?

DR. TANNENBAUM: Now we're getting somewhere! Let's move into this gradually. Start with residuals. Just relax, breathe slowly in and out through your nose and tell me your projected income from residuals this year.

PITCHER: A muh-muh-muh-muh-m-muhhhh. . . .

DR. TANNENBAUM: Easy does it, Mr. Graeslki. Don't force it. Let's try some free association. I'll say a word and you say the first thing that comes to your mind. Here we go: "Mother."

PITCHER: Manager.

DR. TANNENBAUM: "Million."

PITCHER: T-Shirts.

DR. TANNENBAUM: (*almost falls off his chair*) A muh-muh-muh-m-MILLION? Do I infer correctly that you make a *million dollars* off the sales of your T-SHIRTS?

PITCHER: (*sheepishly*) Yep. And afore I tell you what I makes off mah posters you better take yourself a Valium, Doc.

DR. TANNENBAUM: We're running out of time. Just tell me your total income and maybe I can help you.

PITCHER: O.K. Here goes. You cain't say as I didn' warn you. (*sighs cathartically*) Four million, three hunnert 'n twelve thousand bucks 'n eight cents.

DR. TANNENBAUM: (*scratching a note for the first time*) I had no idea of the magnitude of your problem, Mr. Graelski.

PITCHER: Help me, Doc.

DR. TANNENBAUM: I'll do my best. You'll have to see me five days each week when you're not on the road. And I'm afraid I'll have to charge you my critical care rates.

PITCHER: If you kin get rid o' the onerous burden of my income, Doc, I'd do anythin' for you.

DR. TANNENBAUM: (*punches some figures on his pocket calculator*) Anything?

PITCHER: Why, I'd give you the shirt off mah back!

DR. TANNENBAUM: (*glances at his figures*) Oh you will, Mr. Graelski, you will.

28 THE SHORTSTOP WHO CAME IN FROM THE COLD

WHAT Bobby Fischer was to American chess, Yuri Propovich was to Russian baseball. It may come as a surprise to Americans that Russia could produce anything resembling a baseball player, let alone a world-class shortstop. Yet, the record speaks for itself: in the nine years Propovich played for the Kharkov Redsox (1928-1937), he batted .416, initiated 803 double plays, and made only 12 errors.

Unfortunately, one of those errors resulted in the Redsox losing the final game of the Socialist Republic League playoffs to the Omsk Cranes in 1937. Propovich was sent down to the Salt Miners, a farm club in Eastern Siberia where he remained on the active roster for the next twenty-seven years. In the early winter of 1964, during a blizzard, he reportedly died on third base. But not before he had written his memoirs.

Yuri Propovich's *Play Ballski!* is the first book on Russian baseball to be smuggled successfully out of the Soviet Union. (The delightful English translation is by Miriam Taylor Swift, who occupies the Chair for Soviet Baseball Studies at Radcliffe.)

In the heady days (Monday through Wednesday) of the Bolshevik Revolution, the early commissars were ready to take on any challenger to Marxism. What better way, they reasoned, to humiliate the bloated capitalists of the United States—e.g., Babe Ruth—than by beating them at their own game? Leon Trotsky is cited by Propovich as the "Little Father of Soviet Baseball."

According to Propovich, Trotsky developed a fondness for America's pastime in New York where, in 1917, he spent a few months during his second exile. On his return to Russia after the Revolution, he carried among his personal effects a bat, an infielder's glove, and a baseball autographed by Honus Wagner. Trotsky incurred the wrath of Stalin by throwing the ball only to Lenin when the three of them would step outside to "toss the old *pillski* around."

Stalin, a born third baseman, taught himself the rudiments of baseball from a manual his agents pilfered from Trotsky's apartment. His misinterpretation of the phrase "sacrifice the runner home" led to the disappearance of the entire top of the batting order of the Minsk Cubs in the summer of '23.

Under the charismatic leadership of Trotsky, the first Commissar of Baseball, the Socialist Republic League flourished. Since admission was free, as well as compulsory, the proletariat attended the games en masse. At first bored, the Russian people eventually took advantage of the leisurely pace of *baseballski* which allowed them to play chess in the stands almost without interruption.

Discovered by one of Stalin's scouts, Yuri Propovich, a barefoot Ukranian from Georgia, tried out for the Odessa Smelts in the spring of '25. He hit a home run his first time at bat and, according to a sports writer for the *Odessa Tribune*, "covered the territory between second and third like the Ural Mountains." In his report to Stalin, the scout observed that "he moves to the left good, like a Bolshevik should."

Propovich's gracefully arching batting style owed a great deal to his wielding a scythe since childhood in the wheat fields of Georgia. At the same time, he perfected his throwing arm by hurling rocks, tomatoes, and eggs at the horse-drawn carriage of Count Alexy Smirnoff, his landlord.

To the American baseball fan, it may come as a shock to learn that Yuri Propovich was initially signed by Odessa as a food and beverage vendor. The collectivist spirit of Soviet baseball conferred as much prestige on a leather-lunged vendor as it did on a leather-gloved shortstop. As a result, Propovich spent his first three years in organized Soviet baseball trudging through the stands, hoarsely shouting, "Fresh caviar! Hot blini! Get your cold Stoly here!"

The enormous ruble-volume of his sales quickly put him on Stalin's subversive list. It was only through the intervention of Commissar Trotsky that Yuri was traded to the Kharkov Redsox and allowed, at last, to play *ballski*.

Propovich fondly recalls the opening day of the 1926 season when Stalin threw out the first bomb. Yuri received only a flesh wound, and finished the day five for five (a homer, three troikas, and a double). Despite a manifest weakness for vodka and ballerinas—or because of it—Yuri went on to become a superstar of Soviet baseball.

After Propovich's exile to Siberia, and Trotsky's flight to Mexico, baseball virtually disappeared from the Russian mainland, only to surface after WW II in the Caribbean. According to Propovich, Fidel Castro, a middling—some would say meddling—right-handed pitcher, was originally trained as a Soviet mole. Castro's mission was to get signed on as a New York Yankees minor league prospect, with eventual graduation to the majors. He was programmed to pitch a no-hitter, or at least a shut-out, in a World Series game, at the completion of which he was to strip off the top of his Yankee uniform, exposing a red Karl Marx T-shirt underneath.

In the light of subsequent events, Propovich concludes that the Soviet Missile Crisis in Cuba was nothing more than a cover-up for the fact that Castro had a 55 m.p.h. fastball, a rising sinker ball, a clothesline curve ball, and a dry spitball.

29 SOVIET WEIGHTLIFTER'S URINE TESTS POSITIVE FOR KRYPTONITE

THE pervasive use of steroids and cocaine by athletes has given new meaning to the terms "bullpen" in baseball and "nose guard" in football. If the trend continues, the average major league second baseman will weigh 310 fatless pounds by 1992 and earn $6 million dollars a year, a fifth of which will go to his coke dealer, a fourth to his steroid doctor, a third to the IRS and the rest to the Betty Ford Clinic. For the average nose guard, you can multiply these figures by two.

The origin of substance abuse in sports can be traced to Popeye's conspicuous consumption of spinach during his boxing matches with Bluto in the Thirties. Barred in his declining years from further spinach-doping, Popeye desperately turned to asparagus but flunked the urine test.

The introduction of more sophisticated additives into sports began in Madrid during the late Sixties when bullfight promoters began beefing up their *toros* with steroids. In response to these mega-bulls, the terrified matadors began snorting cocaine before stepping into the ring. The upshot of this drug frenzy was the repeated occurrence in the bullring of a phenomenon known as *el toreador desinflado*, or the flattened matador.

In 1978, Poland conducted a study on members of its national chess team to determine if steroid injections could improve their abysmal performance. During a match with Yugoslavia, each beefed-up Pole, whenever he was threatened with checkmate, swept all the pieces off the board with his left arm and knocked out his opponent with his right fist. This endgame strategy was so effective in staving off imminent defeat that it became known as the Polish Defense.

The first suspicion of steroid use by a female athlete occurred at the Montreal Olympics in 1976 when Elke Holtz of East Germany tossed her javelin for what would have been a world record if it had not pierced the Goodyear Blimp. The six-man crew of the blimp bailed out, inaugurating the traditional parachute jump into Olympic Stadium.

No discussion of drug abuse to improve performance would be complete without mention of the beloved circus elephant, Dumbo. Revisionists are beginning to suspect that Dumbo's success in flying was not merely a function of the configuration of his ears coupled with an overweening self-confidence. A study of FBI files on Dumbo, made available through the Freedom of Information Act, reveals that the flying pachyderm had a $40,000 a day cocaine habit—and this, mind you, in 1941 dollars. Following his first film, Dumbo entered the Betty Boop Clinic, after which his career took a permanent nose dive.

Although Dumbo clearly was able to get high on cocaine, considerable doubt persists over whether anabolic steroids truly enhance athletic performance or merely provide the cosmetic appearance of prowess. For the past five years, six male gorillas at the San Diego Zoo have been administered steroids in an effort to resolve this controversy. Last month an animal rights group obtained a restraining order, forcing zoo officials to cease and desist further experimentation and to release the primates into a wild environment.

As a result, the great apes were signed on as offensive linesmen for the Chicago Bears. In their first game against the Detroit Lions, they were collectively penalized 286 yards for holding.

30 THE 37TH ANNUAL EXERCYCLE RALLY

*T*HE hit of this year's Exercycle Rally in Helsinki was a 1940 Wellington stationary bicycle built for two. Made in wartime England, the Wellington was designed to provide simultaneous fitness for the two-man crew of the Mosquito bomber. Arranged in a British square on the airstrip, the Wellington exercycles, most historians agree, gave the RAF that indefinable edge, culminating in Churchill's pudgy-fingered "V" at the end of the Battle of Britain.

An unsung skirmish in the Battle occurred in the spring of '41 when the *Luftwaffe* parachuted 120 men strapped to Fokker exercycles into southern England under cover of darkness. When the RAF flyers mounted their Wellingtons for their predawn workout, the Germans struck. Still strapped to their Fokkers and pedaling at 90 rpm in perfect synchrony, the Germans attacked with pistol fire from behind underbrush bordering the aerodrome.

The Brits, astride their Wellingtons, dodged bullets from the enemy Lugers and fired back with machine guns mounted under the handlebars. When the smoke cleared, the eighty surviving Germans were found seated on their idle Fokkers with their hands in the air. Following this debacle, the Germans never again used the exercycle as an offensive weapon.

Besides a vintage Wellington, the 37th Annual Exercycle Rally also featured a restored Japanese Kamikaze exercycle used in the Battle of Okinawa. From a height of 800 feet, Japanese dive bombers released the Kamikaze exercycles and their riders over American aircraft carriers. Most of the exercycles were blown out of the sky before they could hit the deck, but one landed on the bridge of the U.S.S. Independence and bounced 200 feet in the air. Despite crying "Banzai!" and pedaling furiously, the Japanese warrior landed in the water.

"What was *that*?" asked the Captain.

"Japanese exercyclist, sir!" responded a lieutenant.

"Damn the exercyclists," said the Captain, almost bringing off an immortal line. "Full speed ahead!"

Today's exercyclists are almost as fanatic as their predecessors from the Land of the Rising Sun. The publication in Japan twenty years ago of "Zen and the Art of Exercycle Maintenance" sparked an international craze for the sport that has not yet peaked.

The United States alone boasts over 12,000,000 registered exercyclists most of whom spin their wheels in the privacy of their bedrooms. Over the years, out of sheer boredom, large numbers of exercyclists have taken to meeting at rallies where they can scrutinize each other's calf muscles and swap information about the latest accessories.

The French, for instance, have come up with a wine rack that straps to the handlebars and hooks up to the tension dial that controls the wheel's resistance. The more wine the exercyclist drinks, the lower the resistance. By the time the rider has consumed the last bottle, he is wheeling freely and feeling reely. Or to translate partially from the French, "What he has gained in heart, he has lost in liver. *Vive la Résistance!*"

Also unveiled at this year's rally in Helsinki was the Polish gasoline-powered exercycle, the *Combuski*, which actually frees the rider from the burden of pedaling. The *Combuski*, in effect, transforms the exercycle's driving force from manpower to horsepower. Sales are reported to be brisk in Krakow.

The Russian entry, the MIG XR 3, is more labor-intensive than Poland's *Combuski*. The MIG XR 3 is equipped with a power-train assembly connected to the wheel. In the spirit of "power to the people," the rider can provide heat and electricity for his apartment as long as he can stay in the saddle and pedal.

When he dismounts, off go the TV, the room lights, the stove, and the refrigerator. The Russians estimate that if they can hook up 5,000,000 MIG XR 3's to a central power station, they can put an exercyclist on the moon. With the reduced gravitational pull on the lunar surface, the Soviets would take a giant spin for mankind with a tenth of the effort required on Earth to achieve optimal aerobic fitness.

The Americans are countering this potential threat with the

top-secret Stealth exercycle. All that can officially be said about the Stealth is that the American booth at the 37th Annual Exercycle Rally in Helsinki appeared, to the naked eye, to be empty. The exercycle, of course was invented in the United States just after the turn of the century. Working out of a garage in Kitty Hawk, North Carolina, two brothers, Wilbur and Orville Wright, converted a circus unicycle into a primitive exercycle of sorts.*

In one-hundred-degree-plus temperatures, they installed a large, pedal-activated fan-blade in front of the wheel to cool off the rider. To prevent the unicycle from tipping over on its fragile stand, the brothers attached two long, wing-like projections to the handlebars, allowing the exercyclist to maintain balance while spinning his wheel.

One night, a neighbor, Stanislaus Zebrzydowski, stole into the garage and, as a prank, attached a 30 h.p. engine to the fan blade. The rest, as they say, is history.

The Wright Brothers' prototype bears only a vestigial resemblance to the modern American exercycle. Thanks to high tech spin-offs from Silicon Valley, it is now possible to monitor and display all of the exercyclist's cardiopulmonary functions simultaneously.

At the first sign of an imminently fatal heart-rhythm disturbance, the exercycle shuts itself off and auto-dials 911 on the mini-phone built into the seat. Should the rhythm disturbance worsen before help arrives, the cyclist suddenly sees his whole life flash before him on the monitor screen, provided he has taken the precaution of programming in his whole life, and updating it, before mounting. Otherwise, he sees a *sample* whole life flashing suddenly before him. This sample whole life is issued by the manufacturer with the disclaimer, "Any resemblance to a person, or persons, living or dead is purely coincidental."

Whether he rides a low-rider exercycle customized in Southern California or a Cleveland Plain Wheeler made in Ohio, the American exercyclist is distinguished by his total commitment to 50% fitness. His red shorts, white Adidas and blue tank top show off to dubious advantage what one English observer has described as " the legs of Apollo, the belly of Bacchus."

*Mostly self-taught, the Wright Brothers began designing and building printing machinery, then went into the business of selling bicycles and later of designing and manufacturing them. *Encyclopedia Britannica*, 15th ed., Vol. 19, p.1032.

"Sure, we like our beer," says Ed Jensen, a fifty-six-year-old exercyclist from Milwaukee, "but (pats his abdomen) the bulk stops here."

Grizzled exercyclists like Jensen have spent decades perfecting their characteristic physiques. "Our biggest fear is to be mistaken for, God forbid, BI—cyclists," says Jensen. "Those skinny twits on their two-wheeled widow makers have no idea of the joys of stationary fitness. The older the bi—cyclists get, the farther they fall behind their young competitors. Whereas, you can *never* fall behind on an exercycle. Of course, you can never get ahead, either—which may not be American, but, hey, that's life."

Ed Jensen is one of seventy-five members of the Milwaukee Sprockettes, a trisexual, unicyclic, multiracial stationary exercycle club that rallies bi-monthly. The Sprockettes, who are often invited to exercycle in Radio City Music Hall, are famous for their precision leg kicks after every third revolution. Only in America. Where the question is increasingly asked, "When will exercycling become an Olympic event?"

"Not till Helsinki freezes over," came the official reply last January from the icebound Finnish capital.

Does this mean that exercycling has finally entered the fast lane? A further clue that Olympic sanction is just around the corner is the allegation by the Milwaukee Sprockettes that the Bulgarian women's team is using hormones. "Look at the legs on them dames!" cries Ed Jensen. "Either they're takin' androgens or King Kong had ten daughters!"

Elixirs of Youth

31 PYRAMID POWER

*According to Engineer Karel Drbal of Prague,
"There is a relation between the space inside a
pyramid and the physical processes going on
inside that space." Drbal stated he had used a
razor blade until it was blunt. After he placed
it along an east-west axis under his accurate,
scale model of the Cheops pyramid, he claimed
the blade became sharp again.*

San Francisco Chronicle

*M*R. David L. Cribbens worked as a stockbroker in a twenty-fifth-floor office on the west side of the Transamerica Pyramid in San Francisco. In the winter of '86, just before his firm moved into the Pyramid, Cribbens was in an obvious state of physical decline.

After fifty-seven years, what little hair sprouted between his ears was snow white. Even at rest, his breathing was labored. When he phoned his clients, they would often remark, "Is this an obscene phone call or is that you, David?"

In short, it was with a well-documented sense of impending doom that he moved with his firm to the Pyramid.

Embalming himself with five martinis every afternoon, Cribbens ceremoniously repaired to his cubicle deep within the Pyramid and muttered "tut-tut" to his secretaries' entreaties that he lie down for a spell. During the calamitous bear market of '87, the end of each day found Cribbens swathed mummy-like in ticker tape with the supplications of his clients to Drop Dead ringing in his ears.

Then, after about nine months in the Pyramid, subtle but remarkable changes in his physical status began taking place. Shoots of jet-black hair began refoliating his scalp. His stride, five martinis notwithstanding, began taking on a semblance of jauntiness. Soon, Cribbens found his eyes wandering from lists of price earning ratios to the 36-24-36 figure of his secretary. Suddenly, he didn't care if the bottom dropped out of the market, so long as the same thing didn't happen to Ms. Wentworth.

Last month, Cribbens dropped dead, a happy man, while chasing Ms. Wentworth around a copy machine. At his funeral, old friends remarked how marvelous he looked. Most gave credit to the mortician. One guest at the funeral, an engineer who had flown in from Prague, had his own theory.

⬤ 32 SNOW WHITE AT FIFTY

S NOW White turned fifty this year. Disneyland
is celebrating this unsettling event with a
daily parade of regal splendor. As a spectator a few Saturdays
ago, I was happy to see that the old girl, her Prince Charming,
and their horse have aged well. Those Beverly Hills plastic surgeons are geniuses.

Of course, those of us who devour the tabloids are all too
familiar with the Royal Couple's less than fairytale-like career
after their marriage: First, there was Prince Charming's brief
affair with Tinkerbell. ("We're just old, dear friends," sobbed
Tinkerbell in a statement released through her attorneys.)
Then, Snow White sailed through the Betty Ford Clinic. (WHO
PUT THE "SNOW" IN SNOW WHITE? blared the headlines.)

In a show of solidarity, the Royal Couple went on an endless
round of benefits for the Animated Wildlife Fund. Next, they
were forced to throw open their Enchanted Castle in Disneyland to the public, owing to prohibitive property taxes. One
night at Spago's, Snow White threw a fit of jealous rage over the
sudden fame of her younger sister, Vanna. Recently, Snow
White was devastated by the bankruptcy of her chain of one-
hour photo shops. ("SOME DAY MY PRINTS WILL COME!"
SOBS SNOW WHITE.)

Despite the trouble she has had living happily ever after,
Snow White is faring much better than the Seven Dwarfs. You
don't hear much about the Dwarfs these days. I did, over drinks
at Chasen's one night with the seventy-three-year-old—but
still spry—Jiminy Cricket, who made the mistake of swearing
me to secrecy.

After closing down their jewel mine, the Seven Dwarfs

entered the Screen Actors' Guild Retirement Home in Hollywood and proceeded to squander their fortune on outrageous medical interventions. They fell into the clutches of Donald Duck, M.D., a Los Angeles quack, who took it upon himself to "cure" them of their various "maladies."

First, he injected the dwarfs with human growth hormone, causing them to achieve an average height of five feet, ten inches, which robbed them of a considerable amount of their charm.

Next, he diagnosed Sleepy as having narcolepsy and prescribed amphetamines; as a result, Sleepy hasn't had a good night's snooze in over forty years. He phones late-night talk shows and brags, until he's cut off, about the pivotal role he played in the assassination of the Evil Queen in the spring of '37.

Sneezy was given antihistamines which cleared up his nose but aggravated a chronic prostate condition. His fellow dwarfs call him Wee-Wee behind his back.

Dr. Duck diagnosed Grumpy as "unipolar depression" and prescribed a mood elevator which transformed Grumpy's behavior from comically querulous to blandly affable. He is frequently asked to sit on the dais at Orange County republican fundraisers.

Dopey was yoked with a diagnosis of "learning disability" and sent to a remedial school where he was taught to speak and read. He became an intellectual, fell under the spell of Nietzsche, and bored his fellow dwarfs to distraction by pontificating on the theme, "God is Dead," following the demise of Walt Disney.

Happy was diagnosed as "manic-depressive, manic type," and placed on a permanently sobering dose of lithium carbonate. As a result, he was able to land a part-time job as a clerk in the Anaheim branch of the Department of Motor Vehicles.

Dr. Duck had the effrontery to label Doc an "impaired physician." True, Doc in his declining years developed a mild dependency on Snickers and Mars Bars. Using the "cold turkey" method, the fraudulent feathered physician, himself addicted to Cold Duck, ordered Doc put in restraints. Doc was brutally withdrawn from chocolate bars, and force-fed a modified Pritikin diet which broke his spirit.

But Dr. Duck's most egregious commission of malpractice was his insistence that Bashful attend a male empowerment seminar. Three weeks later, Bashful stormed into the Screen

Actors' Guild Retirement Home, flashed an elderly nurse, and decked three L.A. cops before he was subdued. He now fritters away his twilight years with young blondes and old scotch at Beverly Hills "A" parties where he likes to pick fights with the likes of Kirk Douglas and Sylvester Stallone.

Snow White, during a recent visit to her beloved dwarfs, was shocked at their transformation. She complained bitterly to Dr. Duck, who promptly diagnosed her as suffering from a "Cinderella complex."

That night Snow White lovingly prepared and served to her adoring husband a memorable *canard à l'orange.*

⊂● *33* HARD TIMES

*I*N 1976, the sudden failure of San Francisco's only sperm bank, Chartered International Cryobank, sent shock waves through the male population. According to a front page story in the *San Francisco Chronicle*, the frozen assets of two hundred Bay Area depositors were liquidated overnight due to a fatal oversight in temperature control at the vault on Market Street.

Interviewed by a *Chronicle* reporter, wiped-out sperm bank president Robert Quinlan, Jr. reminisced about the early days of his ill-fated project. Looking about for a fail-safe depository, he chanced upon an Army surplus missile silo in Nevada outside of Sparks. According to Quinlan, he could have snapped up the silo for just seventeen thousand dollars, but backed down for want of an economical means of shipping Northern California sperm to Nevada.

In my humble medical opinion, Quinlan's slippery problem could have been solved by an interstate pipeline. Of course, no one consulted me. London's Linear Sperm Accelerator would have had minimal environmental impact. My preliminary sketches (which are unprintable) depict, in scale, a simple polyvinal erection, as it were, two hundred and seven miles long, crossing into Nevada just north of Truckee before penetrating the frigid silo at Sparks.

Quinlan's strenuous efforts to avoid using the word "masturbation" in his promotional literature led to one near-tragic incident, as reported to the *Chronicle*. Quinlan learned that instead of implementing the M word, veterinarians readily collect sperm from horses, sheep and cattle by means of an "electro-ejaculator." (If you think I'm making this up, write the *Chron* or ask a vet.)

With great expectations, Quinlan and a physician drove to the School of Agriculture at Davis, California, in order to try out the device first hand. They soon discovered "one big drawback" in the instrument. "In order to ground it," explained Quinlan, "you had to put a steel rod up your anus."

The anonymous physician, who has joined the ranks of such research martyrs as the first laboratory technicians to handle the anthrax bacillus, volunteered to try the electro-ejaculator on himself. Despite painstaking preparation, the good doctor "almost electrocuted himself," according to eyewitness Quinlan. (The doctor was not available for comment, but one can easily imagine that his hair, standing as it did on end thereafter, and his eyes, with their permanently startled gaze, spoke volumes.)

Quinlan faced an appalling legal barrage from the two hundred depositors whose holdings had vanished overnight. Unhappily, in one of his brochures, he had more or less promised each depositor five hundred thousand dollars insured protection. (When asked how his client could wriggle out of this one, Quinlan's lawyer responded, "No comment," but was privately overheard to mutter, "Oy.") In what must have been, arguably, the first example of "deep-pocket" involvement in a case of spermicide, the insurance company demurely went belly up. As a result, Quinlan was left holding an unsecured stainless-steel drum called a "Dewar's (pronounced *do-ers*) flask" containing trillions of spermatazoa which required for their hibernation a temperature of 321 degrees below zero. Presumably, one of the penalties for early withdrawal from a sperm bank is frost-bitten fingers.

To this day, no one knows if any spermatazoa remain viable in the court-sealed Dewar's flask. If you ask this observer, it sounds like a case for Geraldo.

Appetite
Suppressants

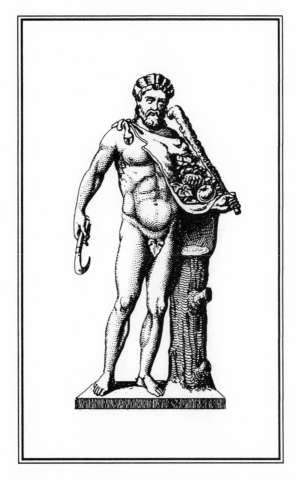

34 TWENTY-FIVE YEARS OF EATING DANGEROUSLY

*F*OR the past 25 years, I have dined at least three times a week at Rod's Hickory Pit, located in the Golden Gate Lanes bowling alley on San Pablo Avenue in El Cerrito. If you crave *nouvelle* or California cuisine, by all means come to Rod's—open 24 hours a day—and you've come to the wrong place.

If you love perfectly fresh Icelandic cod grilled over mesquite, please ask a waitress at Rod's for this dish. Within thirty seconds, four Richmond cops, each weighing in excess of 210 pounds, will catapult you into the parking lot. ("You want mesquite, buddy? Try one of them artsy-fartsy Shay Pansies in Berkeley!") One of the recurrent joys of dining at Rod's is watching an effete yuppie in a three piece suit tossed effete first out the front door.

Rod's is located in the demilitarized zone just south of the warring city-states of Richmond and San Pablo. Rod's is where the black ex-con from Richmond and the blue collar redneck from San Pablo can sit down and enjoy pan-ethnic ribs with a better than 50-50 chance of walking out alive.

Unlike the yoo-hoo bunch of yahoos at Trader Vic's, the clientele at Rod's does not table hop. The inter-table tension at Rod's is so thick it can be cut with a knife and the only reason it isn't is those four Richmond cops sucking ribs in the corner booth.

Sure, the Richmond cops are tough, but when you consider their beat, they have to be. After all, a dark corner of the parking lot at Rod's was the scene of the murder of Rod himself eighteen years ago: shot through the heart by a thief as he got into his white Eldorado. The creep got a week's receipts and was never caught, but four heavily armed cops can always be found inside Rod's after dark, just in case the murderer should ever stroll in and announce: "I did it. I killed Rod Cotton. Top of the world, Ma!"

Since her husband's demise, Mrs. Cotton has managed the Hickory Pit with consummate skill. Her annually renewed white Eldorado is parked just outside the front door, where a spotlighted sign reads:

THIS SPACE RESERVED FOR MRS. ROD COTTON
ALL OTHER VEHICLES WILL BE TOWED

Towed, my foot. If any misguided, myopic customer chances to park his car in her hallowed space when Mrs. Cotton is off-duty, the four Richmond cops rip the vehicle into bite-sized pieces with their bare hands and serve it to the Fat Man in the front booth.

Aside from the Jackson Pollack-like spatter of blood stains on the floor, the decor of the Hickory Pit is undistinguished: metal-lic hood over pit, leatherette booths, long formica counter for the coffee and cigarette set. (At Rod's you are given a choice between the Smoking Section and the Heavy Smoking Section.)

During the twenty-five years I have closely observed them, the waitresses at Rod's have come and gone, but happily their white, mini-skirted uniform with the orange apron tied in a provocative bow at the back has remained. And although Rod's waitresses range in age from eighteen to sixty-four, I haven't seen, in more than two decades, a bad pair of legs. I have, in fact, had better luck with the legs on the waitresses than with the ribs on the plate.

Oh, there was a time during the Kennedy era when the dark, smoky ribs were juicy, crispy, and insanely delicious, order after order. Under LBJ, you'd get a gristly, underdone slab from time to time (about which you'd dasn't complain to the Texarkana waitresses). With Nixon, the ribs continued to deteriorate, but were so covered up with barbecue sauce that you were at least spared the sight of them. I can't seem to recall how the ribs were during the—was it Gerald?—Ford interval. But then came Carter and you couldn't get a glass of ice water without asking for it with a toothy grin and the ribs were so bad you were tempted to come back to see if they could possibly get worse and you did and they could. Now, let me tell you about the ribs under Reagan. So-so. A week after Bush was inaugurated, I asked a waitress for "just a splash of sauce" and she had me tossed into the parking lot.

Besides ribs, other items emerging from the hickory pit include turkey, beef, ham, and pork loin—all marvelous at least two or three times a decade (but never on Mondays). For a total pig-out, you can order a "Combination Plate" of ribs, ham and pork loin garnished with barbecue sauce, roast beef, and French fries. I have calculated the caloric content of this single dish to be in excess of 9000. I have seen frail young men sit down to the "Combination Plate" and have to be pried out of their booths with Jaws of Life at meal's end.

Of course, watching what the other customers are doing to themselves is part of the morbid fascination of eating at Rod's. For example, I've observed that a favorite late-night repast of hefty middle-aged men who wear baseball caps is a large vanilla shake plus a double order of fries buried under a lava flow of sauce. The waitresses refer to this order as "Nine-One-One" and sure enough, when the big guys have vacuumed their shakes dry, licked their plates clean, and clutched their chests hard, a blinking police ambulance awaits them in the parking lot to whisk them to the Coronary Care Unit at Brookside Hospital just down the road.

Those of you possessed of an ironclad stomach and a bulletproof vest will find Rod's Hickory Pit to be on the cutting edge of high-risk dining. Take it from me. After eating at Rod's for twenty-five years, I have become the Fat Man in the front booth. And let me confess something else: A two-door, 1976 Pinto is not the toughest thing I've been served there. (You won't find cars listed on the menu. If you want one, or a part thereof, ask the waitress for the "Catch of the Day.")

Rod's Hickory Pit. 11498 San Pablo Ave., El Cerrito. All major credit cards laughed at. Service: excellent. Ambience: hazardous. Food: to die over.

35 THE POST-MODERNIST SANDWICH

*L*AST week, the cafeteria of the San Francisco Museum of Modern Art exhibited six *croque monsieur* sandwiches prepared in 1886 for the Eighth Impressionist Exhibition in Paris. Mistaking them for the sandwich of the day, cafeteria patrons gobbled up three of the priceless artifacts before museum guards and paramedics could intervene.

At the same time, the De Young Museum restaurant displayed two delicate pieces of chicken teriyaki and a side order of tempura dating from the Tokugawa Period (1603-1867). On loan from the Brundage Collection, the chicken and tempura (incorrectly spelled "tempera" in the museum catalogue) have been ascribed to Chef Hideko Watanabe. But seasoned museum *knoshers* point out the flawed glaze on the drumstick and credit the work instead to one of Watanabe's disciples, Saburo ("Two Fingers") Asakawa, best known for his pioneering efforts with a stone-sharpened knife over a teppan grill.

Meanwhile, the Palace of the Legion of Honor is getting ready this month for the long-awaited Treasures of the Hermitage Snack Bar. Smuggled out of Russia in a sealed railroad car, the pre-Revolutionary delicacies have already been exhibited in Rome, Paris, New York, and Boston. At last word, the pelmeni have held up well, but the blini in sour cream are in dire need of restoration.

The recent interest shown in museum food was sparked by the twenty-fifth anniversary of the appearance of Pineapple with Cottage Cheese on the restaurant menu of New York's Museum of Modern Art. East Coast critics fondly recalled the initial outrage of art patrons at the hideous clash of colors: the cadmium yellow pineapple slice, the titanium white mound of cottage cheese, and the alizarine-crimson maraschino cherry. One critic pointed out that the Pineapple with Cottage Cheese is the only item in the permanent collection of the MOMA for which a "Do Not Touch" sign has not been necessary.

It wasn't long before a traveling exhibit entitled, "Food Like MOMA Used to Make—And Still Does," began touring the United States. Long-suffering patrons of museum cafeterias were elated to learn that such neglected classics as Egg Salad Sandwich, Pea Soup, and Tapioca Pudding were being hailed as still-life masterpieces.

Inevitably, prices began creeping up. Last March, a cold roast beef sandwich donated to Philadelphia's Rodin Museum by the Arby Family Trust was listed at $80.00. A croissant from the Louvre, appraised at $300, was auctioned at Sotheby's but bidding was halted when the auctioneer absently took a bite out of the item.

Currently on display at the Salvador Deli in Madrid's Prado is a retrospective of American fast food. Attractively mounted in pastel styrofoam, a Big Mac, a Whopper, a Fajita Pita, and a Western Bacon Cheeseburger drew large, enthusiastic crowds, but garnered lukewarm reviews. The consensus was articulated by *La Prensa's* restaurant critic who concluded, "It's art, but is it food?"

36 FROM CORKAGE TO CABBAGE

*I*F a restaurant permits me to bring in my own wine for a modest "corkage fee," what is to prevent me from bringing in my own entrée? If I can save eighty bucks by thrusting two bottles of Spinelli Brothers Asti Spumante into the hands of the sommelier, why couldn't I save another forty by bringing in a chuck roast from Safeway?

After a dozen phone calls, I finally found a very expensive restaurant desperate enough for business to allow me to bring in my own chuck roast provided I precooked it, wrapped it in aluminum foil, and smuggled it into the restaurant in a shopping bag from Neiman-Marcus.

Done.

With a flourish, the waiter presented me and my lovely companion with menus. With a wink, I handed him the shopping bag containing two bottles of sparkling wine and a chuck roast.

"Ah, you must be the gentleman who requested corkage and roastage."

"The very one," I said. "Waiter, our special tonight is a London broil overcooked by my mother, Mrs. London, and basted in a sauce comprised of a tart, domestic ketchup and a crisp envelope of dried onion soup. All your chef has to do is pop it in his microwave for ten minutes. And would you mind placing my wine in an ice bucket?"

"Very good, sir," said the waiter. "May I suggest we serve the London broil in a bed of buttered new potatoes sprinkled with cilantro?"

"Actually, I threw in some of Mom's canned stringbeans, so the potatoes won't be necessary."

"Very well, sir, but we'll have to charge a vegetage of fourteen dollars for the stringbeans."

"A fourteen dollar vegetage?" I said. "That's an outrage! But I'll agree, if you'll just add a little oil and vinegar to these lettuce leaves I've sneaked in."

I handed the waiter a morning *Chronicle*.

"Ah yes," he observed, "inside the *Sporting Green*. I'm sorry sir—we don't provide tossage."

"Can't you just lay them on a plate and simply charge for roughage?"

"Very well, sir."

Our bill totalled only $47.00, including twenty dollars for corkage, ten for roastage, three for roughage, and fourteen for vegetage.

I should have quit while I was ahead. Instead, I asked the waiter to wrap the leftover beef in my Neiman-Marcus bag. He insisted on charging me ten bucks for "canine baggage."

I next made the mistake of informing the waiter that I had already arranged for a taxi to pick us up after dinner. He added twelve bucks to my bill for cabbage and left me an insulting fifty cents in tippage.

37 THE JEREMIAH TOWER OF JACK-IN-THE-BOX

*D*UANE Neely, the head chef of Antioch's Jack-in-the Box, shocked fast-food cognoscenti last week by accepting the position of *saucier* at the prestigious McDonald's on Shattuck Avenue in the heart of Berkeley's Gourmet Ghetto. Widely acknowledged as the Jeremiah Tower of fast-food chefs, Neely had trained under the legendary Ralph "Buns" Smith of Der Wienerschnitzel in Auburn. (Some say that Buns Smith is the Wolfgang Puck of fast-food chefs; others insist that Wolfgang Puck is the Buns Smith of California cuisine.)

In any event, Neely then served briefly as pastry chef at the San Leandro Carl's Jr., but quit after four months when he had mastered the art of microwaving the apple turnover, the only pastry appearing at the time on CJ's menu.

His reputation soared at Antioch's Jack-in-the-Box where his rendition of the Fajita Pita—his signature dish—attracted connoisseurs from as far away as Martinez. Rumor has it that he left Jack-in-the-Box for McDonald's—"from the frying pan into the fire," as he puts it—when management introduced chicken as an alternative to beef in the Fajita Pita.

As one seasoned fast-food diner described it from his bed in the Coronary Care Unit at Moffitt Hospital, "Mr. Neely was famous for the deft way he sautéed lean strips of beef in his Fajita Pita. I mean, beef was his medium, like marble was Bernini's. Then here comes this joker shouting over the intercom for three orders of *chicken* Fajita Pita. Well, as you can imagine, Mr. Neely was deeply offended and refused to fill the order. Pretty soon, cars in the take-out lane were backed up for three blocks. By the way, could you possibly run out and sneak me back a Jumbo Jack, hold the onions?"

Neely's groupies are already lining up at the Shattuck Avenue McDonald's where he began work as *saucier* on Tuesday morning. They say he hasn't quite mastered the intricacies of McDonald's Secret Sauce yet, but is already turning out a superb Sweet & Sour and a more than passable Hot Mustard to accompany the traditional Chicken McNuggets.

His affiliation with chicken, he assures his friends, is merely expedient. Insiders say that he has set his sights on doing for the Big Mac what he did for the Fajita Pita.

Outspoken in his insistence on absolutely fresh-frozen ingredients, Neely continues to be in demand at gourmand seminars around the Bay Area. Next Sunday he is appearing at a $2.59-per-head fundraiser for the Save the Whopper Society to be held in the smoking section of Burger King in El Cerrito. His subject: Whither Wendy's?

Among the most ardent fans of Neely's cooking are not a few legendary Bay Area slow-food chefs. The latter have understandably traveled incognito to the various establishments where Neely has held forth. During his triumphant tenure at Jack-in-the-Box in Antioch, a petite lady, costumed as a bowler, sat down one night and scarfed two Fajita Pitas, a large order of french fries, a Taco Salad, and a small chocolate shake.

Although it has never been proven that the mysterious diner was Alice Waters, several customers observed her reach into the pocket of her rayon sateen jacket, pull out a small plastic envelope and furtively sprinkle nasturtium leaves over her Taco Salad.

Neely himself prefers to dine at Stars, Chez Panisse, and Square One, but can't afford to.

38 NEVER SMILE AT A BUSBOY

*T*HERE'S a restaurant in San Francisco that's so good and small and expensive, that before it will consider your reservation, you are asked to submit a résumé. I must say I was put off by this requirement at first, but the more I thought about it, the more sense it made. I don't want to sit down at any event costing more than $200 per person without having some assurance that I am surrounded by people of similar taste, breeding, VISA credit-limit, and savoir-faire.

In my résumé, which ran to seven single-spaced typewritten pages, I emphasized those qualities of mine that I felt made me uniquely worthy of consideration for a reservation for two at 9 P.M. on a Thursday evening.

I pointed out my near-impeccable table manners that won me designation as "First-Runner-Up" this year in the International Fork-Lift Competition sponsored by the *Académie d' Étiquette Francais*. In the event the winner should forfeit his title—as did last year's champion when he was revealed eating a chili dog in the centerfold of an old issue of *Truck Diner* magazine—I myself would then become "Monsieur Fork-Lift of 1989."

As M. Fork-Lift, I would do everything in my power to enhance the cause of world peace, to make baton twirling an olympic event, and to bring about an international understanding that the salad be served *after* the entrée.

In my résumé, I also disclosed the name of my tailor, the makes of my cars, my unlisted phone number, and which of my three residences I'd be willing to have a lien placed against in the event my check bounced. As requested, I attached a copy of my 1040 form. I then mailed in my résumé and hoped for the best.

In less than a week I was asked to appear for my interview. The panel of judges consisted of the maître d', three captains, an assistant pastry chef, the sommelier, and a waiter. For over two hours I was grilled—perhaps "basted" is the more appropriate term—on the finer points of dining at an Incredibly Expensive restaurant.

They wanted to know if I had ever smiled at a busboy. Would I send a sommelier back to the wine cellar for a deficiency of polish on his medallion? If I were choking on a piece of venison in truffle sauce, would I signal for the Heimlich maneuver to the maître d' if it was obvious that he was preoccupied with extracting a scintilla of lint from his sleeve?

I answered the questions as best I could, shook the gloved hands of the judges and went home. Three weeks later, I received a notice by registered mail that the judges had carefully reviewed my qualifications and regretted to inform me that "you do not quite make our kind of restaurant."

On the other hand, my lovely companion (whose passport photo I was required to attach to the résumé) was "welcome *any* time." It was like a scene out of *A Star is Born* and I was Norman Main!

She was a good sport about the whole thing; I bankrolled her nine-course feast and she agreed to bring back a sample of each dish in the restaurant's famous Gucci Poochy Bags.

Let me tell you—the food, even warmed over, was sensational.

I'm permitted to re-apply for a reservation in three years. I'm already booked for basic training at Ernie's, L'Etoile, and Le Trianon. I've enrolled in a correspondence course in "Butter Knife Strategies" at the California Culinary Academy. I'm having my name legally changed to "Donald Trump."

Next time around, I'll have those judges eating out of my hand, or my name, for the time being, isn't Oscar London.

*T*HE first rule of Winesmanship, as played in three-star restaurants, is SEND BACK THE FIRST BOTTLE. Do not explain your decision to the wine steward. Simply glance at the label and ask that the bottle be returned to the cellar at once. This maneuver may win you *as many as 12 points* at the outset.

First of all, it virtually demolishes the wine steward before he can score any points with his simple little two-pronged corkscrew (as opposed to the elaborate, multi-jointed apparatus he knows you use at home). Secondly, it allows you to finish your double martini in peace. To be sure, the wine steward may earn three points by saying "thank you" in response to your directive that he retreat with the first bottle. Furthermore, if his complexion turns neither burgundy red nor *chenin blanc* while he thanks you, he picks up another four points. But, at worst, you are already *five points ahead*, by simply observing rule number one: SEND BACK THE FIRST BOTTLE.

The second rule of Winesmanship is BUTTER THE CORK. You have been presented by the wine steward with your bottle. Sacrificing three points, you permit him to remove the cork. You pick up the cork, regard it indifferently, and proceed to butter the dry half. This tactic will so unnerve your opponent that, likely as not, he will miss the brim of your glass completely while pouring your trial dose, and *you have earned another six points*.

The third rule of Winesmanship is GARGLE THE TRIAL DOSE. Pick up the glass but do not sniff the bouquet. (I can't tell you how many points are lost during sniffing to the wine steward with his "sommelier than thou" attitude.) Do not swirl the first sip or "chew" it. Instead, gargle it. Quietly, of course, but with head cocked resolutely back and with eyes fixed intently on some imaginary—or, preferably, real—spot on the ceiling. You may then proceed to swallow with the satisfaction of having picked up, *without challenge*, another eight points.

The third rule of Winesmanship is ANNOUNCE "FOURTH SQUEEZING, THIRD HARVEST, LACKLUSTER YEAR," AFTER SWALLOWING THE TRIAL DOSE. This rule applies whether you are dealing with a Mouton Rothschild '28 or a Mountain Red '88. No wine steward in his right mind would challenge you on a point of squeezing or harvesting. Body or clarity, perhaps. Squeezing and harvesting, never. Now, he may decide to attack you on the year. If so, you respond by biting off the buttered half of the cork, munching it reflectively for a while and finally conceding, "You have a point there." A POINT! You have gained *four points*, given away *one* point, netting you *three* points.

You are within two points of forcing the wine steward to award you his medallion. But, be careful here. Your opponent is growing more dangerous by the minute.

The fourth rule of Winesmanship is IGNORE THE WINE AFTER THE TRIAL DOSE. With a curt nod, you allow the wine steward to complete the filling of your glass. *That's as far as he gets.* Two hard-won points for him, but he has fallen into your end-game trap.

You proceed to ignore the wine. Concentrate, instead, on the water. Drink the water with increasingly heightened enthusiasm. Summon the busboy in loud tones to refill your water goblet. Demand that the busboy confess the water is "bottled" rather than merely "on tap." Compliment the busboy on the remarkable clarity of his ice cubes. Meanwhile, *don't touch the wine.*

If the wine steward should happen to step forward and ask, "Is anything wrong, sir?," oblige him with, "Not at all! Not at all! I say, while I have you here, may I trouble you for some more water? Your busboy is doling out the stuff as if it were so much *eau froid.*"

If the wine steward does not know the French translation of "cold water," you have already won the game. If the wine steward is conversant in French or if he fetches the water and pours it abundantly over your head, you have suffered a major setback. You might be able to salvage a point by observing, "You're a better man than I am, Gunga Din," taking care, of course, to pronounce the name, "gun-ga dan."

The fifth rule of Winesmanship is GRAB THE BOTTLE AND CHUG-A-LUG IT À LA SODA POP. Leave a small amount in the bottle before replacing it on the table. Turn to the wine steward and remark, "I like to leave a wee bit for sedimental reasons." You are back in competition.

The sixth rule of Winesmanship is PEEL OFF THE LABEL FROM THE BOTTLE AND AFFIX IT TO THE BROW OF THE WINE STEWARD. If the wine steward has been properly trained, he will concede defeat by flipping his cork and frothing at the mouth, not unlike a properly opened bottle of fine champagne. On the other hand, if he refuses to give up, he may politely suggest that you step outside with him into the alley behind the restaurant.

The seventh rule of Winesmanship is IGNORE ANY SUGGESTION MADE BY THE WINE STEWARD.

40 THE BREAD LINES OF BERKELEY

*I*T is 9:30 on a foggy Tuesday morning in Berkeley. A line of shivering, half-starved men and women stretches from the front door of Acme Bread Co. across a parking lot jammed with blue Volvos.

Skinny as Italian breadsticks, the pale bearded men stare vacantly as the line inches forward. The women, too, are skin-and-bones; their frail running shorts and flimsy tank tops offer no protection from the cruel wind, the piercing cold, the vacant stares of the pale bearded men.

Bread. They are waiting for bread. They are lined up, hollow cheek to absent jowl, waiting for designer bread—sourdough rye, crusty Levain, spicy Fougasse, and rye raisin Rabbits.

"Just a slice or two of sourdough rye," they tell themselves, "maybe with a little cream cheese, then back to 800 calories a day, so help me Pritikin."

The gaunt young men and women have pounded the pavements since daybreak in their down-at-the-heel Nikes. Running for their lives, they have suffered an average of six miles apiece. Who can fault these underweight overachievers for expecting a crust of bread as reward for a jog well done? Starved to near perfection, giddy with hypoglycemia, bowed by osteoporosis, they beg the question: Was ever a bread line during the Great Depression so sorry a spectacle as this one?

A warm scent of rising sourdough suddenly fills the parking lot. A collective groan of bread lust rises from sunken chests. A physicist faints. An alert internist hops over the prostrate form of the quantum theorist to advance one place in line. No one protests. A congregation of more than sixty Berkeleyans and no one protests! It is the Acme effect.

As a public service, Acme Bread throws open its doors to Berkeley's underfed masses for a limited time each day. Having filled its substantial commercial orders, Acme offers its leftovers at a charitable mark-up requiring no more than two Brinks trucks to haul off at day's end.

The trouble is, there is never enough bread to satisfy more than a handful of supplicants. The net result is the infamous Berkeley Bread Riots.

The pale bearded customer embraces the last sale of the morning—a warm oval of pumpernickel—and starts to run a down-and-out pattern across the parking lot. He hasn't got a prayer. Before he can make it to his Volvo, he is engulfed by an enraged mob of empty-handed gourmets. By the time the Berkeley police arrive, all that's left of the last customer is a hank of hair lightly sprinkled with bread crumbs.

The commotion in the parking lot outside Acme is not lost on the illustrious proprietress of Fanny's Café next door. When informed that the masses are revolting and demanding bread, Alice Waters declares, "Let them eat *croque monsieur!*"

The ravenous mob surges inside Fanny's. In a gesture at once magnanimous and nostalgic, Fanny's rolls back its prices to those of the previous week. The ascetic crowd breaks its Pritikin vows and tears into perfectly grilled ham-and-cheese sandwiches on Acme's fabled *pain de mie*.

Elated, the bread rioters hoist Alice on their bony shoulders and sweep into Kermit Lynch's wine shop next door. Another brouhaha erupts over whether the '85 *Lavantureaux Petit Chablis* surpasses in bouquet that of the '85 *d'Epiré Savennières "Cuvée Spéciale."* The Bread Riot has escalated into the War of Noses.

When glass starts to fly, the police rush in wielding night sticks as long and hard as day-old baguettes. The bruised rebels spend the night in Berkeley's upscale slammer where they are kept in salutary confinement and fed only bread and water— rye raisin Rabbits and Perrier with a twist.

41 A CHILD'S GUIDE TO FRENCH COOKING

T *he events portrayed in this affectionate memoir of Julia Child are either true or false, depending on the reader's ability to tell a base canard from a basted one.*

At the age of seven, Julia Child ran up to me and cried, "Oh, Uncle Oscar! Why are all the great chefs *men*?"

Bending down, I scooped her up in my arms, gave her a big hug and sat her down on my lap. "There, there, Julia my Child," I said, "you mustn't generalize so. Certainly not all the great chefs are men. Let's see. There's Ralph, there's Jeremiah, there's Wolfgang, there's Marvin, Umberto, Nick, Seymour, Chang, Joel, Larry, Pierre, Stanley—by golly you're right! All men!"

Poor little Julia burst into tears and pounded her fists against my starched apron.

"It's not fair! It's just not fair!" she cried.

"Please, my little cream puff," I said. "You're getting my apron dirty."

"Oh, I'm sorry, Uncle Oscar—I was just starting a batch of mud pies Provencale when I saw you appear magically on our veranda."

Yes, I am Oscar Child London, beloved uncle and magic chef, as it were, of Julia's childhood. Of course, Child is her married name, but, if my memory serves me correctly, it was also her maiden name. At any rate, I'll always remember Julia as a Child.

Frankly, I taught the kid everything she knows.

During her summer vacations in the Thirties, she served as my waitress in a modest cafe I owned and operated on Truck Route 18 outside of Trenton, New Jersey. I called it Oscar's Grill, but, to Julia's considerable dismay, my most loyal patrons referred to it as the Grease Rack.

I always had the feeling Julia was not happy with her job. She had this thing about French cooking which, *entre nous*, your average truck driver was not about to swallow. Every now and then she tried to slip in a croissant when a customer was expecting toasted white bread.

"Julia, Julia, Julia," I would lament, sounding not unlike Cary Grant. "These are tired, hard-driving Americans. They don't want continental cuisine. They want *trans*continental cuisine."

In the summer of '36 I turned the cafe over to Julia while I attended the National Convention of Fry Cooks held in the ballroom of Pete's Place in Kenosha, Wisconsin. This, of course, was 1936, B.C.—Before Cholesterol—and how we loved our food! As I recall, no less than eight delegates grabbed their chests before the conclusion of the kick-off breakfast and pitched headlong into their bacon and eggs.

While I was away, Julia, a natural-born French chef, ignored everything I'd taught her. As best as I can piece together the facts, she insisted on serving fluffy omelettes with *fines herbes* in place of my eggs Oscar over easy. She substituted lamb kidneys in caper sauce for my six rashers of underdone bacon. Crisp potatoes *lyonnaise* replaced my alabaster hash browns. Demitasses of *café filtre* were her pallid substitute for my mugs of corrosive black coffee.

The upshot of Julia's debut was that my customers began to defect to Elmer's Cafe down the road. Poor Julia. In a last-ditch effort to recoup her losses, she tried to serve a die-hard customer a plate of *crêpes Aunt Jemima*. Somehow, she'd managed to unearth a bottle of my 180-proof bootleg brandy, *Chateau Capone '31*. She poured about eight ounces of the stuff over the pancakes and placed the heady dish before the dubious patron. To his horror, she ignited his breakfast with a match, crying, "Bon. . . bon. . . BON FIRE!"

The flames, I am told, shot forty feet in the air, finding their final height through a nine-foot hole burned in my grease-spattered ceiling. In less than three hours, Oscar's Grill deep-fried itself to a crisp.

Despite my efforts, Julia was inconsolable. She ran away from home and entered a French convent. Fortunately for television fans of Julia Child, the head chef of the convent was Sister Alizette, who had devoted her life to mastering the art of

American cooking. In culinary circles, she was known as the Frying Nun.

Fed up with Spam, malts, and French fried potatoes, Julia sailed home on the first boat, retired to her kitchen in Connecticut and emerged, years later, in your living room.

That's the gospel truth, or my name isn't Oscar of the Waldorf.

42 O COME WITH ME TO THE WINE COUNTRY!

*B*EFORE choosing a female companion for my annual trip to the wine country, I invariably consult my wife. Despite the weight of past experience, she has, to date, always stepped forward at the last minute and volunteered.

Our marriage, like many a fine California burgundy, was the by-product of some squeezings in a Napa Valley vineyard during the autumn of 1963—a vintage year for redheads, some of you may recall. In an effort to recapture our days of wine and roses, I plan, each fall, a sentimental weekend of lazy motoring through the scented vineyards of Napa Valley. My itinerary allows for an escape, now and then, from the merciless sun into the cool cellars of not more than thirty wineries.

In a recent speech delivered inadvertently to the neighborhood at large through an open window in our kitchen, my wife contended that my sole interest in a winery resided in the tasting room. Although, in the equal time allotted me, I managed to refute this charge (the phone calls of congratulation clogged our answering machine for days), the truth is, I approach a winery with a single overriding question: "What's in it for me?"

Admittedly, more often than not, I find the answer somewhere in the tasting room.

The wine tasting room! The finest flower of California's Adult Education Program! A one-room schoolhouse—with no tuition!—where the ignorant palate can learn to tell a Pinot Noir from a Zinfandel! A Grey Riesling from a Pinot Chardonnay!

"But you never know when to quit," my wife points out.

"A little learning is a dangerous thing," I remind her.

On a crystalline Saturday morning in September, having resolved our differences with a firm handshake, we hopped into our wine-dark fastback and drove the fifty miles to Napa Valley from our home in San Francisco.

We ate a brown bag lunch on one the tables studding the wooded grounds of the Monte Cordova Winery just south of Rutherford. The tall trees, the soft breeze, the stone walls of the winery—all worked their magic. By the time we had drunk the last of the Chianti I had brought along as a little surprise, we were once again that blissful young couple of twenty-five years ago, gamboling and frisking in the vineyards.

Turned back by a sign reading, "Gambolers and Friskers: Keep Out!," we retired to the Monte Cordova tasting room. The handful of tourists at the small bar chose to ignore my merry cry of "Set 'em up, boys! Drinks are on me!"

Things went smoothly enough through the aperitifs and into the burgundies. It was during the dessert wines that I felt the familiar wifely tug at my elbow. After giving her my familiar glassy stare, I suffered the icy blast of her whispered announcement that she would wait for me in the car.

Two drinks later, I yielded to an overwhelming impulse and shouted, "I can lick any man in the house!" I looked about me and made an agonizing reappraisal of the muscular development of the male tourists at the bar. With what he later described as "a simple left hook, followed by a right cross," a construction worker from San Jose, making his first tour of the wine country, sent me to the stone floor for a count of ten.

I was carried to my car on a large plaster shield bearing the heraldic crest and familiar label of the Monte Cordova Winery. Seeing me snap awake, my wife instructed the shield bearers to pour me into the bucket seat behind the steering wheel. On second glance, she had me decanted into the passenger's seat.

As she drove off, we settled back to endure one of the more profound silences of our long marriage. Finally unable to restrain myself any longer, I exclaimed:

"Just look at this scenery! The red and gold grape leaves! The sturdy pickers in the fields bent at their task! The sun on the hills! Why, you can smell the very wine in the air!"

"That's your breath, darling. Open your window."

After visiting seven or eight minor wineries off the highway, we spent the night in Coma—a somnolent village north of St.

Helena. We awoke refreshed at 2:00 P.M. and set out for our favorite winery, Mont St. Pierre in the hills west of Calistoga. Sober for the time being, I was once more in the driver's seat.

When they spotted our familiar fastback inching up their driveway, the good friars of Mont St. Pierre began scurrying about, locking gates and boarding windows. I stepped on the gas and beat them to a side entrance. We were inside the tasting room before you could say, "Johannesberg Riesling!"

The Mont St. Pierre white table wines exceeded my fondest expectations. I was about to pick up my sixth sampling of their Gewurztraminer when my gaze fell on an open bottle of champagne standing grandly aloof on a shelf behind the bar.

"I think I'll try some of your champagne," I said, pointing to the bottle.

"I don't recommend it," said Brother Lucien.

"Why not? Reluctant to part with some private stock, eh, Friar?"

Without another word, he poured me a brimming glassful of the bubbly nectar. Approving of its assertive bouquet, I sipped it slowly, appreciatively.

"Lovely, just lovely," I murmured, putting down my empty glass. "Boisterous and impulsive, but not at all naive. A great champagne!"

"Wrong," replied Brother Lucien. "A good liquid detergent."

"Liquid detergent?"

"Yes. We keep it in that old champagne bottle to use when we wash out our visitors' glasses."

For a full ten minutes, my wife tells me, I simply stood there, growing red in the face and foaming at the mouth.

After we bade the jolly friars adieu, I found myself in a weak bargaining position to protest my wife's decision to call it a day.

"Honey, just one more teensy-weensy winery for the road, please? You have no idea how that detergent cleared my head."

"Shut up, bubble brain, and keep your eye on the road."

Not a very flattering comment, but at least it showed she recognized who was in the driver's seat.

Homeward bound, we were heading south through Napa when I slowed down to admire the towering, ivy-covered walls of Esterhazy Winery. One of the oldest establishments in the area, Esterhazy was famous for its Champagne Brut and its nineteenth century, oak-panelled tasting room. With parched palate, I turned to my wife for a final appeal and discovered to my delight that she was sound asleep. The hearty laugh she had had with the good friars at my expense had exhausted her.

I slowly pulled into Esterhazy's parking lot and quietly got out of the car so as not to disturb my sleeping beauty. I walked up to an elaborately carved door labeled, "Tasting Room."

I opened it and received the shock of my life. In place of Esterhazy's renowned mahogany bar and red-jacketed wine stewards, a row of vending machines stood facing the entrance! Crowds of tourists waited in line to deposit their coins—their coins!—in the variously labeled machines. At the touch of a button, the wine of their choice flowed into a small paper cup.

Over the clatter and gurgle of the machines, a recorded voice continuously droned through a loudspeaker:

"Greetings! In order to accommodate our growing number of visitors, we have automated our tasting room. In this way, our guests may have a wide selection of our fine wines literally at their fingertips. Please have your exact change ready. Greetings! In order to accommodate. . . "

Dazed, I walked from one vending machine to the other, staring in disbelief at such labels as:

ESTERHAZY
CABERNET SAUVIGNON
'63. . . 25¢
'59. . . 50¢
'47. . . 75¢

Then I came to the largest machine in the room. Across its front was printed:

Our World-Famous
ESTERHAZY
CHAMPAGNE BRUT
Only $1.00 per Cup

"Et tu, Brut?" I cried, running out of the room and into the parking lot.

My wife was still sleeping in the car. I started to awaken her to tell her of Esterhazy's decline and fall, but the lovely smile on her face so poignantly reminded me of happier days in Napa Valley, that I let her sleep all the way home.

And Now for a
Healthy Dose
of Reality

43 I REMEMBER TODDLE HOUSE—AND THE GLORY THAT WAS GREASE

*D*URING the short, hot summers of my boyhood, I ate out a lot, alone. At lunchtime my mother was usually attending a B'Nai Brith meeting; my father was on the road, selling New Era shirts. Given a choice between cold cuts in the icebox and a hot meal out, I took the lunch money and ran.

In the Forties, I enjoyed a wide variety of cheap, good food in a business district of limited expectations in the largely Jewish suburb of University City, just west of St. Louis. Blondie and Dick's was a bright orange A & W franchise near the Tivoli theater. On a tropically hot afternoon, a foam-capped A & W root beer in a frosted glass mug was as close as you could get to heaven in University City, Shaare Emeth Temple down the street notwithstanding.

Blondie and Dick, a fiftyish married couple, grilled their hamburgers and hotdogs over charcoal, using beef of an ambrosial succulence—corn-fed beef that is fully appreciated only in retrospect by Midwesterners after they've moved away.

Along with my large A & W, I would order a hamburger *and* a hotdog, to avoid the agony of indecision. With measured bites and sips, I contrived to make both sandwiches disappear simultaneously with the last caramel-scented drops of root beer. An Arabian burp of satisfaction from my Reformed Jewish stomach was my compliment to the chefs.

Another place I frequented was the White Castle hamburger stand near the Wabash train station. Spellbinding vapors of burnt fat and raw onion issued from a vent in one of the castle turrets. At the first whiff of this giddy incense, what boy of nine could refrain from storming the wooden gates of White Castle?

Each White Castle hamburger cost a dime and was boxed in a cardboard container designed to resemble a white castle. The burger and bun were of an inferior quality—a skimpy, half-fatted patty lost inside a pale hemisphere of soggy bread.

What made the Castle enchanted were the onions. Lank, warm strands of raw onion permeated burger, bun and box with a piercing smell that could make strong men cry and pudgy boys sob convulsively. A heavy smear of mustard plus translucently thin slices of sour pickle further covered up the shortcomings of meat and bread.

A White Castle hamburger went fast. One night, in my Uncle Dave's car, I ate seven in fifteen minutes, a feat that astonished my Cousin Arthur, who, after his first bite, had imprisoned his wounded burger for life inside its cardboard castle.

For a change-of-pace roast beef sandwich and salad, I ventured into Club T, a small, dim Italian restaurant next door to the Varsity theater. Marco, the owner, was a powerfully built, darkly handsome man who had served as a corporal in the United States Infantry during World War II. A tinted photograph of Marco broadly smiling in a beribboned uniform was perched on one of the shelves behind his bar. I thought he looked a lot like Cary Grant in the picture, and almost like him in person, his gravy-stained apron tending to mar the resemblance. Except in the picture, I never saw Marco smile.

He would carve my sandwich from a huge slab of perfectly broiled prime beef—"the color of teakwood on the outside and rosewood on the inside," as Richard Condon would have described it. To my muted rage, Marco always served me charred end-cuts shot through with gristle.

Awed by his war record and menacing demeanor, I didn't protest when Marco dumped his throw-away pieces on my sandwich. (He saved the choicer cuts for his preferred customers.) On the plus side, he covered his sins with two slices of excellent Italian bread dipped in natural gravy. So, all told, the sandwich was a little better than half-bad.

The salad was another matter. After placing a small wooden bowl on the counter, Marco created my salad out of the national colors of Italy, using fresh chunks of tomato, bell pepper, and celery. He then roofed over the salad with a latticework of anchovy filets.

Marco probably thought he would drive the nine-year-old kid out of his adult restaurant by repeatedly inflicting anchovies on him. Little did he know that, to me, the taste of anchovies was a sensual delight rivaling the sting of a line-drive hardball caught in the oiled pocket of my Heine Manush fielder's glove.

I was able to survey the laying on of anchovies with feigned detachment—a pose I found impossible to maintain when Marco reached for the "House Dressing." This was an oil-and-vinegar-based elixir corked inside a clear-glass wine bottle. A comingling of spices and other arcane sediments gave the dressing the color of pink Italian marble when Marco shook the bottle. To his credit, he splashed a liberal amount of the tart libation over my salad. I not only ate every shred of anchovy and vegetable, but sopped up the residual dressing with a piece of bread wrenched from my sandwich.

Years later, when I was away at college, my mother wrote me that Marco had shot and killed a customer with a pistol and was sent to the Missouri State Penitentiary for twenty years. I never learned what led up to the shooting, but I suspect it had something to do with gristle.

And then, above all, there was Toddle House. I cannot speak for the scores of Toddle Houses that dotted the map of the eastern half of the United States on the back of each menu. I can only speak for the Toddle House, open twenty-four hours a day, next door to the Varsity theater on Delmar Boulevard in University City, Missouri, circa 1945. This hallowed landmark of my youth was a small wooden building that housed twelve white stools lined up against a long, black counter.

When I had a choice, I sat in the last stool on the right. From this vantage point, I could survey the entire Toddle House operation without swiveling my head and, at the same time, avoid getting sandwiched between two customers.

While I checked the back of the menu to see if the Toddle House empire had founded any new colonies, the counterman interrupted his operation of the noisy dishwasher to greet me with a rural salutation and a glass of water.

"What's it gonna be today?" he asked.

"A hamburger with onions, an order of hash brown potatoes, and a Coke." There they are. My very words. Pure poetry. Often recited through a floodtide of salivary juices.

The counterman drawled my order to the cook who sing-songed back, "One with, and a side of hash." The counterman poured my Coke, ice-cold, from the classic six-ounce bottle into the legendary tulip-shaped glass. While sipping the needle-sharp drink, I watched the spectacle of my food being cooked four feet in front of me. I faced a wall of immaculate, stainless steel refrigerator doors, shelves of thick, white dishware and a central, spatula-polished, silvery grill.

Served on a toasted bun, the Toddle House hamburger, to come right out with it, was not quite as good as Blondie & Dick's. To explain my preference, a technical discussion of Toddle House's covered grill versus Blondie & Dick's open grate would be helpful but tedious. Suffice it to say, the Toddle House hamburger was very fine in its own right. After all, "we mustn't fault Telemann for not being Bach."

The Toddle House hash brown potatoes were, quite simply, the best single dish I have ever eaten. In *From Here to Eternity*, James Jones confers on a mess sergeant the highest culinary decoration by stating that the sergeant's hash brown potatoes "were almost as good as Toddle House's."

Over the few years of my boyhood, I saw many cooks come and go at Toddle House but each one seemed to have mastered the art of the House specialty. In a black frying pan, the cook first heated up an unconscionable amount of Crisco and then went to the refrigerator for a small, white paper bag of diced potatoes. Dropped from a height of six inches, the potatoes hit the hot Crisco explosively. As the half-inch cubes settled down to a sizzle, the cook showered them with paprika. (Paprika was the fairy dust of this dish.) Then, with an always bulging and usually tattooed forearm, the cook began shaking hell out of the smoky-red potatoes. Sometimes the Crisco would ignite and a fountain of blue and yellow flames would momentarily engulf the proceedings. For sheer culinary pageantry, I have never seen the equal of Toddle House.

The hamburger and hash brown potatoes would arrive at my place, steaming. Reflexively, I reached for the bottle of Heinz ketchup and shook big red blobs over the potatoes. Too soon, the last crisp fragment of potato, with its clinging drop of ketchup, disappeared like the final bittersweet note of a guitar sonata by Rodrigo.

The *pièce de résistance* on the Toddle House menu was the chocolate icebox pie. "There you go," said the counterman as he placed before me my order of chocolate icebox pie, wobbly with freshness, the pointed end aimed at my heart.

Topped with whipped cream, the filling was of a surpassingly dark chocolate that rested on a browned graham cracker crust. Oh God. How impoverished by comparison with mine was Marcel Proust's boyhood whose most evocative sensation was the lemony taste of some crummy cookie!

Toddle House, as I knew it, is no more. My brother Bob, on a recent visit to the South, sent me a menu from an establishment that had the cheek to call itself a Toddle House. The menu was a shocking document. No hash browns! No chocolate icebox pie!

You may be able to go home again, but you can't go to Toddle House again.

44 SNOW WHITE AND THE SEVEN HUNDRED DWARFS

I SPENT the finest hours of my declining years of boyhood inside the Tivoli, a third-rank movie palace looming above a shop-worn business district in St. Louis. Each weekend the Tivoli's matinée bulged with the works of the minor cowboys, the early Batman, and the late Boris Karloff.

On rare occasions, a Technicolor magnum opus was featured, long after closing at one of the first-run houses. Such an event occurred on a Sunday afternoon in the fall of 1938 when *Snow White and the Seven Dwarfs* opened at the Tivoli. A full two hours before showtime, a block-long line, three to four feet high, had formed before the ornate box office. About a third of the way back, stood my Cousin Arthur and I.

The magical appearance of the box office girl behind her window sent a spasm of joy writhing down the line. For a long time, she just sat there, expressionless: Snow White in her glass coffin. Then, Prince Charming, decked out in the red and gold uniform of Head Usher, opened the box office door and bent tenderly over her shoulder. Lo and behold, she came to life!

Ecstatic, we dwarfs, dressed in our Sunday best, trooped by and showered her with silver quarters. (Mine represented a whole week's allowance.)

In the crush before the usherette at the main entrance, a boy no older than six, wearing patched blue jeans and a shredded T-Shirt, tapped me on the shoulder. He turned out to be the forward scout of a ragged procession of have-nots, who, through the years, have singled me out in crowds.

Under the noses of the usherette and my equally austere cousin (who was shaking his parents down for six bits a week at the time), the boy offered me a dime if, just before the show started, I would walk down to the far exit on the right and push open the door for him. Finding myself deficient in popcorn funds by exactly ten cents, I agreed instantly.

What followed was the only inside job, to my knowledge, ever committed in full view of 700 witnesses.

In all fairness, I must say to my cousin's credit that he gave me ample warning before he disowned me. For ten minutes, Arthur did everything in his power, short of giving me a dime, to dissuade me. But the thought of that thin boy, and his thin dime, waiting out there for me, was too compelling.

"I'll be back in a minute," I whispered to Arthur as the theater lights dimmed. The aisle leading to the Exit slanted down so steeply that I suddenly found myself hurtling past the point-of-no-return despite having resolved, in transit, to call the whole thing off.

As I pushed open the clangorous metal door inside the hushed theater, a blinding shaft of sunlight spotlighted the scene of the crime. I felt something metallic being pressed in my left hand and something wiry shoving past me. Instantly, a pointy-fingernailed grip about the ear lobe riveted both of us to the spot.

In the guise of an usherette, the Evil Queen herself had us in her clutches. During our forced march up the center aisle, I caught sight of my cousin staring at the unparted curtains on the stage. In urgent need of a character reference, I called out his name. Arthur began looking for something under his seat.

The usherette released us under the marquee. Rubbing my ear, I looked up at her and asked, "Has the feature started yet?"

"If you ever set foot inside the Tivoli again," she cackled, "I'll call the police!"

After drying my eyes with the handkerchief my mother had tied my ticket money in, I found myself standing alone. Inside the palm of my left hand, I discovered a moist penny. My partner had welched on me!

For several minutes I paraded my inflamed ear and puffy eyes before the box office girl. At last, with a regal crook of her index finger, she summoned me before her. She gave me an enchanting wink and picked up the first Princess telephone ever used in St. Louis. She spoke the magic words and—lo and behold—Prince Charming appeared, smiling in the doorway!

With his glowing wand, he led me to my former seat. Cousin Arthur, masterfully playing Grumpy to my definitive Dopey, acknowledged my return by transferring his box of popcorn from the hand nearer me to the other.

I GREW up in St. Louis during the prime of Stan "The Man" Musial. In 1943, the Cardinals still played at Sportsman's Park, a grimy stadium reeking on a hot day of all our fathers' sweat and cigar smoke—a tired ballpark echoing the murmur of a slack-jawed crowd aroused from time to time by the crack of a base hit or the cry of "Cold beer here!"

In 1943, Stan Musial was a seasoned Cardinal of twenty-three, while I was a boy of twelve. Now we are both converging on senescence. "The Man" is sixty-eight. The boy is fifty-seven. That, of course, is baseball.

The Saturday game between St. Louis and the New York Giants began at one P.M. In contrast to the grubby stands, the playing field of Sportsman's Park was pristine. Phosphorescent white lines marked off the diamond; the major league dirt of the infield looked like pure ground cinnamon. And the grass! William Wordsworth never trod a meadow beside Lake Windermere so unashamedly green as the outfield of Sportsman's Park.

The first two Cardinals—Musial and Slaughter—ran out on the field to take their positions. Under the tropical sun, their white and red uniforms were as dazzling as a pair of dice skipping over bright felt in Reno.

I wore my souvenir Cardinal cap and sat with my father just behind the box seats between home plate and third base. My father, like the century, was in his early forties. He was a shirt salesman for a company that, like my father, would grow fat during the War.

For some of our fathers, the action during a baseball game was not confined to the field. Placing a bet at Sportsman's Park required a certain amount of stealth and a rudimentary knowledge of the territory. The Jewish bookmakers patrolled our section between home and third. The Irish gamblers were strung out along the first base line. The black gamblers were bunched in the right field bleachers. The Germans, high in the upper deck behind home plate, did not gamble; they owned the ball club, the ballpark, and the brewery.

Moe the bookmaker, his handsome face distorted by a wad of hot dog inside his right cheek, paused in the aisle just below us. He talked, necessarily, out of one side of his mouth, taking bets with the speed and precision his two sons would show after the War in biochemistry and physics.

To my horror, my father leaned forward, tapped Moe on the shoulder and placed a five-dollar bet on New York to win. (I never sang for *my* father, either.)

By the third inning, the Cardinals led six to nothing and Musial was already two for two, a double and a triple. (The ballistics of a Musial extra-base hit were those of the M-1 Garand rifle.)

After the first inning, a succession of New York pitchers trudged to the mound, refused blindfolds and stood facing the bats of Musial, Slaughter, Kurowski, and Cooper.

The Cardinals were still at bat with no outs in the third, when an enormous white cloud a mile above the pitcher's mound suddenly darkened to a visiting-team gray. A muted growl of thunder indicated that some of the gods, like my father, had bet on the Giants to win. Out of left field, a cool breeze washed over the stands, chilling the hearts of beer vendors and giving wing to hundreds of mustard-stained napkins.

In its effort to compete with the War and the Cardinals as a topic of conversation, the weather in St. Louis could be quite assertive. A shaft of lightning struck the top of the flag pole in center field, singeing the Stars and Stripes and, below it, the banner of the 1942 World Champion Cardinals.

Seconds later, a heart-stopping crack and bam of thunder filled the stadium. Before its echo disappeared, the rain was upon us. The drops were fat and cold and they displaced from the hot expanse of grass an overpowering green fragrance.

Like mourners around a headstone, the four black-garbed umpires gathered at home plate. Thunderstruck, they stared at the flash-flooded infield and gazed up at the heavens. Pooling their collective wisdom, they concluded it was raining cats and dogs and called off the game.

My father and I joined the stampede for shelter underneath the stands near Grand Avenue. Cigars soggy, shoes ruined, all bets off, the huddled masses compacted themselves in the great democracy of the half-drenched. For twenty minutes the storm continued to gather strength.

As I stood watching the rain, I became vaguely aware of a new presence beside me.

My father—may he rest in peace, all bets on opposing teams forgiven—draped an arm across my shoulders and said,

"Show my son your ring, Stan."

I looked up at the unmistakable, hawk-beaked profile of The Man. Hatless, batless, Musial was dressed in an unsullied beige suit, a white-on-white shirt, and a silver-and-brown-striped tie. His tan, bone-dry loafers gleamed with a bottomless shine imparted by legions of shoeshine boys who had knelt at the foot of their hero. His sharply parted dark hair was still wet from his locker room shower. The Man Himself stood with us mortals under the grandstand, waiting for a break in the storm.

"Show my son your ring, Stan," my father repeated in a louder voice.

The left-handed hitter smiled and slowly extended his right fist. On the fourth finger was his World Championship ring—a glittering prize of the Cardinals' victory, the year before, over the Yankees. An effulgence of gold, diamonds and rubies, Stan's ring seemed to light up our entire section underneath the grandstand.

Nowhere in the canons of baseball is it ordained that a Jewish boy must kiss the proffered ring of a Cardinal, but for a fleeting moment on a rainy day in St. Louis forty-five years ago, I was tempted.

Musial blushed at the growing adulation surrounding him. Suddenly, he stepped out into the rain and hailed a taxi. It did not appear to me that he got wet.

46 FARBLONDJET

Farblondjet *(pronounced: far-BLAWN-jit)*
. . . Lost (but really lost), mixed-up,
wandering about without any idea where you
are. The Joys of Yiddish, *by Leo Rosten*

SOME of the unluckiest people I've ever met are those who come up to me and ask for directions. I must admit that I *look* like someone who knows his way around. I shudder to think how many errant travelers to San Francisco have been taken in by my hawk-like gaze, my purposeful stride, my general appearance of the Man Who Can Lead You Through the Jungle. These are but the protective mannerisms of a lost soul—a Wrong-Way Corrigan inadvertently hopping the Atlantic, an Inspector Clouseau wheeling about and stepping into a stairwell, a lemming marching resolutely *away* from the sea.

My almost total lack of a sense of direction has plagued me all my life. In grade school, trusting teachers would summon me to their desks and hand me classified documents to take to the Principal's Office. Search parties would have to be sent out to rescue me from the labyrinth of corridors through which I was wandering, *farblondjet.*

In the summer of '46, at a Boy Scout Camp in Irondale, Missouri, I was elected to the Order of the Arrow, a semi-secret, honorary society. My initiation rites included a solitary march at night to a promontory known as Red Rock, eight miles from camp. I was permitted to use flashlight, map, and compass but was forbidden to speak to anyone. The next morning I was found trudging a dusty back road *sixteen miles* from Red Rock, having walked the correct distance, 180 degrees in the wrong direction.

Despite my cautious advance on Red Rock, I was inducted into the Order of the Arrow in a midnight, torch-lit ceremony reminiscent of the ascension to the Round Table of Sir Galahad.

The emblem of the Order was a red arrow on a white sash worn diagonally across the chest. Needless to say, on the night of my apotheosis, I wore the emblem across the wrong shoulder with the arrow pointed toward the ground instead of the sky.

It's not that I've marched to a different drummer through my life, but rather that I've marched to the *same* drummer, but in a different direction.

Before my younger brother's wedding in St. Louis in 1954, I foolishly volunteered to pick up at Lambert Airport an obscure aunt who was flying up from New Orleans. Through blind luck and the kindness of strangers, I managed to find the airport and claim Aunt Ida. (My about-to-be, *long lost* Aunt Ida.)

Getting out of the airport onto Highway 40 involved negotiating a series of elliptical, circular, and figure-of-eight overpasses, detours and off-ramps. My mission: deliver Aunt Ida to my brother's house in suburban St. Louis in time for the wedding at a nearby temple. While Aunt Ida prattled on like Blanche Du Bois with a Yiddish accent ("So how's by Deah Grandma Rachel, mine honey chile?"), I was clutching the steering wheel with the white knuckles and sweaty palms of the *farblondjet*.

An hour after we left the airport, Aunt Ida, regally ensconced in the back seat of my Chevy Bel Air, leaned forward and discreetly tapped me on the shoulder.

"Sweetie," she said, "you should excuse me, but we've just crossed ovah the rivah into Illinois—the wedding's maybe in Chicago?"

Aunt Ida, obviously from a branch of the family not afflicted with hereditary geographic dyspraxia, had correctly observed that I had just traversed the Mississippi River, over Eads Bridge, into East St. Louis, Illinois.

I do not suffer humiliations gladly. A former recipient of the Order of the Arrow, I was forced to appoint Aunt Ida (a total stranger to St. Louis) my back seat driver on our trip back to the arm-crossed bosom of our family. Dressed to the nines and fit to be tied, they were waiting for us at my brother's house. If looks could kill, my brother would still be serving time for fratricide.

Since I was best man (as opposed to brightest man), the wedding could not start without me. In my haste to change into a tux (the guests and the rabbi had been yawning in the temple for an hour and a half), I managed to wriggle, by mistake, into my brother's rented jacket which was two sizes too small on me.

Blind with fury (and afflicted himself with hereditary geographic dyspraxia), my brother Bob easily slipped into *my* ample jacket and the nuptials proceeded without further mishap. (The wedding pictures clearly show the pale, frowning brothers in their ill-fitting jackets, and a radiant Aunt Ida, fresh from her auspicious entry into St. Louis, her ignominious exit, and her triumphant return.)

Somehow, my faulty internal guidance system did not prevent my graduating medical school, but certainly played a role in my choosing Internal Medicine rather than Surgery as my specialty. In 1958, during my second year of hospital residency, I was summarily drafted into the U.S. Army Medical Corps. An instant Captain, I was shipped to Fort Sam Houston in San Antonio for a six-week crash course in the military arts.

It was my good fortune (and that of the nation) that my two-year stint in the Army Medical Corps took place in the interregnum between Korea and Vietnam. One of the most important military courses I was required to take at Fort Sam was Map Reading. The moment I walked into the classroom and saw a fiercely mustached major about to point to a huge map of the training grounds outside of San Antonio, I knew I was in for it. Suffering a momentary auditory hallucination, I could hear my cocky left brain derisively shout "Ha!" across to my cringing right brain.

The final examination in Map Reading was held in the field. Dressed in battle fatigues and armed only with map, ruler, and compass, we were ordered to pretend we were in combat and to come up with an ideal site for a MASH unit in the wilds of Texas. And, oh yes, we were not to work in groups—it was every man for himself. Shades of Red Rock!

At dawn on the morning of the mapping exercise, a jeep dropped me off, as war correspondents would say, Somewhere in Texas. Squinting into the rising sun, I took my first inaccurate reading and tentatively set out on what I have come to call "Operation *Farblondjet*."

That evening, a helicopter finally spotted me by searchlight at 2300 hours. After turning in my heavily notated map to Major Peck, I was first told that I was technically AWOL, and secondly, that I had set up my MASH unit eight miles behind enemy lines.

After being retired, without fanfare, from the Army Medical Corps two years later, I completed my residency training at Stanford and set up my practice of internal medicine in Berkeley. The latter hillside community is distinguished by, among other things, countless roads twisting up through fog into nothingness. At least, this is my impression of the byways of Berkeley when a patient has had the misfortune to insist that I make a housecall at night.

In the legendary April '61 issue of *Holiday Magazine*, devoted to the San Francisco Bay Area, Michael Arlen wrote:

> If you will look across the bay from San Francisco in a northeasterly direction, you will see Berkeley. . . By night, you see an apparently endless band of lights running laterally across the horizon and vertically up into the dark shadow of the hills; a South American religious procession several million strong, all carrying candles, all lost.

On a clear night, you might be able to spot me if you stand on the Golden Gate Bridge and look across the water at the Berkeley hills. I'm in the top row, fifth candle from the left.

47 THE BAREFOOT INTERNIST

I STARTED my practice during Berkeley's Summer of Love in the early Sixties. Since I was the new Doc on the block, my fees were low enough to attract a number of hippies. They turned to me when their alternative therapists and home remedies had failed them. One such couple lived with their three-year-old son in a converted garage behind a large redwood-shingle house near the UC campus.

The mother, it seemed, had caught a severe respiratory infection from her child and the father called to ask if I would make a housecall. (Only in Berkeley would a notion as radical as a housecall be entertained by an internist newly arrived from Stanford.) I examined the patient at her bedside and made a diagnosis of mild pneumonia. I assured her that she would not have to be hospitalized if she agreed to take a ten-day course of antibiotics.

After I answered her countless but pertinent questions about the side effects of my proposed medication, I wrote her out a prescription and packed up my instruments in my black bag.

"Hey Doc," said the husband, "is it okay with you if I work on Becky's foot in case your toxin doesn't work?"

"Sure," I said.

Here was a man with a Ph.D. in mathematics who had dropped out to start a career as a rolfer, iridologist, and foot reflexologist. At the time, I was curious to learn more about these unorthodox disciplines. What better authority could I ask than a practitioner with an I.Q. of 190?

"Elliot," I said, "would you mind demonstrating for me what you do to the foot?"

"Not at all," said Elliot. "Take off your right shoe."

I suddenly lost interest.

"Oh, I thought you might show me on Becky's foot," I said. "It's already bare."

Not only was Becky's foot bare but so was her son's and her husband's as well.

"Take off your right shoe," insisted Elliot.

In contrast to Elliot's torn, faded jeans and unwashed, tie-dyed T-shirt, I was impeccably attired in a dark-blue, three-piece suit of British woolen; a snow-white, button-down shirt; a red silk tie by Hermes; a pair of navy blue, over-the-calf hose, and mirror-polished, black Bannister shoes. Under the circumstances, I felt like a *fin de siècle* British prince paying a ceremonial visit to a jungle hospital in one of the more primitive and exotic colonies of the Empire.

In what could lamely pass for noblesse oblige in the Berkeley of the Sixties, I sat down on a wooden orange crate and removed my right shoe and sock. What emerged in that dim hovel was a blindingly white, immaculately clean foot with newly trimmed, squared-off nails. Elliot, the bearded shaman, knelt at my feet and grasped my pristine sole with his dirty hand.

He stated that he was about to press certain areas of my foot that corresponded to my various internal organs.

Digging the tip of his index finger into the base of my great toe, he said, "Now here's your brain. Tell me if you get dizzy or feel strange in any way, and I'll stop."

Reflexively, his pressure on my foot caused me acute embarrassment, but I did not judge this sensation to be sufficiently disabling to call off Elliot's demonstration.

"Now here's your spleen," he said, pressing on the ball of my foot. "Feel anything?"

Regretfully, I shook my head. From her sickbed, Becky sensed my discomfiture. Coughing politely, she said, "Elliot darling, Dr. London's had a busy day. I don't think we should keep him here any longer than necessary."

Elliot's eyes narrowed in anger. "Becky, I wouldn't be doing this if he hadn't asked for it."

"Oh, he's just showing you professional courtesy," she said, smiling wanly. "You can't possibly think he *believes* what you're telling him, do you?"

Elliot's grip on my sole tightened alarmingly. He thrust up my foot to her eye level. "Look, Becky, do you realize if I apply a great deal of pressure *right here*, I could kill him instantly?"

I have no idea what Becky's reaction was, but I, for one, was disinclined to have a family argument settled over my dead body. Without standing on ceremony, I snatched my foot from Elliot's grasp, pulled on sock and shoe, and bade patient and husband cheerio. With shoelace untied, I beat an unsteady but hasty retreat out of their garage and into my car.

48 GOD BLESS YOUR CHIROPRACTOR

*A*FTER twenty-five years of practicing internal medicine, I have developed a pronounced tic below my left eye from trying to keep a straight face while patients sing the praises of their chiropractors. "So sweet!" "So gentle!" "So inexpensive!"

As a Berkeley doctor, I spend more time than I care to admit protecting my patients from rival therapists—homeopathists, acupuncturists, foot reflexologists, iridologists, rolfers, and (pardon my tic) chiropractors.

Of course, the reason my patients with recurrent back pain hobble off to chiropractors is that, when I treat them, I never lay a hand on them. Instead, I sentence them to three days in bed with a heating pad and prescribe an anti-inflammatory caplet that upsets their stomach. And then I charge them an arm and a leg for a back that still hurts.

Small wonder they bound into my office a month later and unfurl an X-ray film as long as a carpet rolled out for a visiting head of state. "Look!" they exclaim. "My chiropractor let me borrow this X-ray to show you! He found this malalignment down here. He gave me only three manipulations—he's so gentle! And that did it—my back pain's gone! And guess what he charged me?"

In this situation, I have found that a five-milligram tablet of Valium obliterates my tic for almost four hours.

Why did my treatment fail and the chiropractor's succeed? In my bones, I know that his methods are less rational—and potentially more hazardous—than mine. But no matter how much I try to disguise it, my attitude toward chronic back pain is contagiously pessimistic. And my methods are decidedly hands-off. The chiropractor's outlook, on the other hand, is infectiously rosy. And his hands are drawn to my patient's spine like Lionel Hampton's to a xylophone.

When it comes to treating back pain, my caplet is no match for his charisma—my heating pad, not nearly as warming as his busy hands. I'm still waiting for the day when one of my defectors to the chiropractic comes back to me in a total body cast and mumbles through wired jaws, "I shoulda listened to you, Doc."

In the meantime, if my facial tic doesn't improve soon, I may have to ask one of my patients for the name of his chiropractor.

49 ANXIETY IS THE BEST TREATMENT FOR DEPRESSION

*I*N the past year, a large number of patients have been sending me newspaper clippings about something called "Chronic Fatigue Syndrome." Attached to each clipping is a hand-written note implying that CFS is what's been troubling them for months and that it seems odd that *they* should have to inform *me* of the diagnosis.

Sometimes referred to as "The Yuppie Disease," this is a malady I've encountered under various guises for twenty-five years. Truth to tell, young urban professionals are among the few patients who can afford the exhaustive lab tests ordered by their doctor in a futile effort to find out why they're tired all the time.

The usual suspects rounded up by physicians have included the Epstein-Barr virus, the cytomegalovirus, subliminal herpes, covert yeast infections, environmental allergies, and insidious exposures to toxic fumes. In my practice, the usual suspects have almost always been released for lack of sufficient evidence. I tend to agree with clinical investigators at the University of Connecticut who recently concluded that the major causes of Chronic Fatigue Syndrome are anxiety and depression.

A case history in point:

A beautiful young attorney and mother of two informs me that she has Chronic Fatigue Syndrome. Sara, as I will call her, defends her case masterfully, submitting as evidence five articles on the subject clipped from reputable newspapers. She convinces me that before she came down with CFS, she sailed through law school, married a wonderful guy, breezed through her pregnancies, had a terrific career, skied in the winter, and wind-surfed in the summer.

And then, six months ago, Sara caught a cold at a ski resort in Tahoe and has been a physical wreck every since. Her muscles ache, her head spins, her appetite is shot, she coughs all the time, she can't concentrate, and she runs a half a degree of fever every afternoon. She can't sleep, work, or stand her children. She wants to divorce her unsympathetic husband but is too tired to file the papers.

I perform a thorough physical examination on her in my office—completely normal. At her insistence, I draw off prodigious quantities of her blood and spinal fluid and send them to laboratories around the country; I X-ray her chest; I order a thousand-dollar MRI scan of her brain. Everything, except how Sara feels, is perfectly normal.

When I tell her that I can find nothing physically wrong with her, she requests a second opinion from a legendary Professor of Internal Medicine whom her sister, a cardiologist in Dallas, has recommended. Two months and $6000 later, the professor's second opinion concurs with my first.

In the most tactful manner I can summon, I suggest to Sara that she consult a psychiatrist. Now, the fastest way for a doctor to get a Chronic Fatigue Syndrome out of his rapidly thinning and graying hair is to suggest a psychiatric consultation. Sara leaves my practice in a huff.

Over the next several months, I receive requests for copies of her lab tests from a homeopathist, an acupuncturist, a Feldenkrais therapist, an infectious disease specialist, and finally, from an environmental allergist.

Six months after deserting me, Sara makes a triumphant, unscheduled appearance at my office. My secretary barges into my consultation room to insist I take a look at the patient in the waiting room before I hazard letting her into the office.

With some apprehension, I open my outer door to find my former patient smiling beatifically up at me through a portable oxygen tent. Her once luxuriantly full and wavy hair is now close-cropped. A canopy of clear plastic envelops her head and trunk. A small green oxygen tank is strapped to her back where before Sara had carried her plump, pink daughter.

At first, I don't recognize her because of her new hair style and her eschewal of make-up. She sits alone against one wall of the waiting room, having asked six other patients to move away from her because she is allergic to their cologne. When I invite her into my office, she declines, saying that she is sensitive to *my* cologne as well and just wanted to drop by to "say hello."

Sara volunteers that she feels wonderful no thanks to me, is no longer living with her husband (who has the kids), and has given up her law practice. In perfect time with the tic below my left eye, she sings the praises of her environmental allergist.

The latter therapist concluded, after a battery of tests even more elaborate than mine, that she was allergic to just about everything and everyone on God's green earth. In addition to putting Sara in an oxygen tent, her environmental allergist prescribed miniscule doses of an anti-yeast medication which she avers makes her feel like a teenager again.

After waving goodbye to her from outside her tent, I retire to the cave of my consultation room where I write a letter to the patient's sister the cardiologist. The sister explosively intervenes and personally railroads my ex-patient to a psychiatrist who does not wear cologne.

With the help of a tricyclic antidepressant, the psychiatrist eventually draws Sara out of her tent. He convinces her to put her law practice on temporary hold, adopt a live-and-let-live attitude toward her yeast, and return to her family.

Sara also returns to me, the psychiatrist having overachieved. I treat her now, with varying success, for a condition that long before it was called Chronic Fatigue Syndrome was known as Tired Housewife Syndrome.

50 A GRADUAL DESCENT INTO LAS VEGAS

*A*uthor's Note: *Ms. Dayna Macy, the young, beautiful, and talented publicity director of Ten Speed Press, has frequently been forced to play the role of Jewish Mother to me, a middle-aged doctor of medicine and neophyte author of* Kill as Few Patients as Possible. *Among the requests Ms. Macy received for interviews with Dr. London were repeated entreaties from one Mindie Biederman of the* Las Vegas Today *show. Something about Ms. Biederman's approach—for one thing, its resemblance to that of a charging water buffalo—alerted Ms. Macy to warn me that, under no circumstances, should I say yes to Ms. Biederman should the latter try to contact me directly. Needless to say, when Ms. Biederman managed to get me on the phone, I said yes immediately. My ensuing appearance on the* Las Vegas Today *show inspired me to write the following confession.*

16 October 88

Re: Mindie Biederman and the *Las Vegas Today* show.

Dear Dayna,

Ignoring your flattering appeals to my sanity and intelligence, I flew to Las Vegas Friday night from Oakland. (In other words, from No There to No Tomorrow.) Mindie Biederman's plea that I appear on her *Las Vegas Today* show quickly broke through my veneer of skepticism and exposed 200 pounds of narcissism.

Departure was delayed two hours due to the first October rainstorm over Phoenix in recorded history. The rainstorm, to the best of my knowledge, was not the fault of Mindie Biederman, but every freak of nature that followed was.

I had called Mindie Biederman, Inc. several times during the week to confirm my presence on her show, only to get her "answering service." Since you and I know that Mindie Bieder- man on the phone poses as her own secretary, production man- ager, gofer, manicurist, and executive vice president, I cross- examined the "operator" of her "answering service" mercilessly. The latter finally convinced me that the real Mindie Biederman, if she existed, was either "down with a cold," or "out of town," or both.

Since *Las Vegas Today* is broadcast "Live from the Gold Dust Hotel," I had booked the best room in the Gold Dust at the sus- piciously modest rate of $38 a day. After the two-hour delay and the one-hour flight, the Boeing 737 began its gradual descent into Las Vegas through an overhanging cloud of cigarette smoke and angst. I walked three nautical miles through the unspeakably glitzy airport to a cab whose driver, when he heard me announce "The Gold Dust Hotel," gave me a look of pro- found pity as if I were a dark, shiny bug who had just cried, "The Roach Motel and step on it!"

I will not depress you with a description of my room—one of 800—which, I will only say, smelled like a hastily vacated Marl- boro den. A voice that identified itself as that of "Mindie Bied- erman" aroused me from a halcyon coma at 8:30 a.m. to wel- come me to Las Vegas and to instruct me to appear on the "mezzanine" of the hotel at 1:30 p.m., a half-hour before "Show Time."

I had taken the precaution of wrenching an oxygen mask from a compartment above my seat on the plane and so was able to make it through the lobby-casino of the Gold Dust where, cranking 500 slot machines, stood the extended family of the woman whose picture graces the cover of "White Trash Cooking." (An incessant ringing of electronic bells in the casino was either the din of jackpots or of smoke alarms.)

I took a cab to Caesars Palace where I had an excellent break- fast of corned beef hash in the shadow of a full-scale reproduc- tion of Michelangelo's David. So the trip shouldn't be a total loss, I won $160 at a blackjack table whose kindly white-haired dealer reminded me of my Uncle Irv in St. Louis.

At 12:30, back to the Gold Dust, where I asked several employees for directions to the mezzanine. Blank stares. "I'm appearing on Mindie Biederman's TV show, *Las Vegas Today*." More blank stares. Finally, a security guard who resembled a serial killer in a sheriff's uniform, took me by the shoulders and, ignoring my OSCAR LONDON, M.D., W.B.D. name tag, said, "Mister, I think you should try in back of the second-floor cafeteria where Mindie Biederman puts on her radio show."

RADIO Show?

Dayna, Darling, did you get the distinct impression, as I did, that the Mindie Biederman show was a *TV* production? Oh Fanny, why did this St. Louis kid ignore all that New York wisdom of yours?

The cafeteria on the second floor (nee mezzanine) was a large room whose decor was Early Oakland Bus Terminal. A zoftig, middle-aged woman who identified herself as Mindie Biederman materialized through the vapors emanating from warming trays of leftover meatloaf in the near distance. She looked like my sickly Aunt Rachel, Irv's wife, complete with fever, cough and inedible meatloaf.

After introducing myself, I asked if other "guests" on her "show" came to Vegas expecting to appear on television rather than on—no offense meant to the venerable medium—radio. She feverishly denied that she purposely gave the impression of producing and hosting a live *television* show. Instead, she claimed, she presided over a *radio* show with a live audience. She pointed to 50 empty folding chairs sagging before us. "They used to let me use the lounge downstairs," she explained wistfully.

"But you said the show would be videotaped," I reminded her.

"Yes, and that'll be fifty dollars," she reminded me, pointing to a teenager manning a beaten VCR camera mounted on an arthritic tripod just south of the meat loaf. Not one to neglect the sinker when I've already gobbled up the hook and the line, I had—yes, Your Honor—agreed to purchase a videotape of the "performance."

At this point I became intrigued by the anecdotal possibilities of this fiasco and decided to see it through, with an option to toss Mindie Biederman over the "mezzanine" railing.

"So this is a live radio show you put on," I said agreeably.

"Actually," she confessed, "a high school football game is preempting my time today so we're taping you for next week's show." She pointed to an LBJ look-alike seated before a tape recorder from which snaked two frayed cords with attached black fuzz-ball microphones.

It was 1:50, ten minutes before show time, and the "live" audience now began trickling into the room. I put the word "live" in quotes here to indicate that the average age of the audience appeared to be eighty-six.

Mindie was now coughing like Violetta in the last act of *La Traviata*. She seemed exercised over the fact that her second guest on the show, André Astor, had not shown up. As you can see by the enclosed flyer, I was booked to "appear" with André Astor and Oscar the Talking Dog. Mindie had contrived to have me, Oscar the Talking Doc, appear as second banana to Oscar the Talking Dog. And the latter was a no show.

At one minute before show time, damned if every seat in the place was filled. Mindie whipped out a copy of *Kill As Few Patients As Possible* that looked as if Oscar the Talking Dog had been chewing on it for a month. Here's the most bizarre part—she really loved the book and had literally memorized it in preparation for her broadcast. In fact, she was the best-prepared interviewer I've met since I began doing talk shows. At two o'clock, her genuine cough disappeared and Mindie, the woman of a thousand voices, turned into a silver-tongued pro.

The people in the "live" audience suddenly became lively. And darling. They kept me on my toes for an hour with intelligent questions and gave me laughs Robin Williams would envy. You can see and hear for yourself, if the tape ever arrives.

Halfway through my hour, André and Oscar the Talking Dog tiptoed into the cafeteria. André was clearly miffed at having to wait for the end of my gig and later gave Mindie hell for giving him the wrong time to arrive. When my segment finally expired, André and Oscar took the stage. André, a rather handsome man who looked to be an old thirty-five or a young forty-eight, announced to the audience that he was born in France to a family that had been in show business for 250 years. I believed him about his family's profession but I know a German accent when I hear one.

Oscar the Talking Dog is a live basset hound trained to keep his mouth shut. In fact, André revealed that Oscar was a "she." (So André the Frenchman was a German, and Oscar the Talking Dog was a bitch. By this time, nothing surprised me.)

What André has done is affix to Oscar an elaborate, false, lower jaw—complete with protruding tongue and perfect teeth—that André manipulates from a wire behind Oscar's neck. André, a rotten ventriloquist, then talks and jaws for Oscar. The illusion is uncanny or, as another Oscar would say, un-canine.

The audience, by acclamation, voted me Best of Show and Oscar the Talking Dog, a poor second.

Today, the Mindie Biederman Show—tomorrow, *The Today Show!*

Best,

Oscar